THE SERIOUS HUMOR OF HARRY GOLDEN

Clarence W. Thomas

Research
and
Editorial Assistant

Shirley Robinson

University Press of America, Inc.
Lanham • New York • London

University Press of America, ® Inc.
4720 Boston Way
Lanham, Maryland 20706

3 Henrietta Street
London, WC2E 8LU England

Printed in the United States of America
British Cataloging in Publication Information Available

Library of Congress Cataloging-in-Publication Data

Thomas, Clarence, W.
The serious humor of Harry Golden / by Clarence W. Thomas; Shirley Robinson, research and editorial assistant.
p. cm.
Includes bibliographical references and index.
1. Golden, Harry, 1902- . 2. Civil rights workers--United States--Biography. 3. Jewish journalists--United States--Biography. 4. United States--Race relations. I. Title.
E185.98.G65T49 1996 305.8'00973--dc20 96-41173 CIP

ISBN 0-7618-0565-6 (cloth : alk. ppr.)
ISBN 0-7618-0566-4 (pbk. : alk. ppr.)

™ The paper used in this publication meets the minimum requirements of American National Standard for information Sciences—Permanence of Paper for Printed Library Materials, ANSI Z39.48—1984

This book is dedicated to all the children, women, and men of good will who fought, as well as those who continued to fight, for racial equality and civil rights for all people.

Contents

Preface

Gone, But Not Forgotten

During the civil rights movement of the 1950's and 1960's, many black and white Americans spoke out against racial injustice and rallied to battle racism and segregation. However, few people were as vocal and diligent in facilitating racial understanding and acceptance as the late journalist and author Harry Golden.

As a northern Jew who relocated to the South, Golden witnessed the suffering and cruelty inflicted upon blacks by southern whites and empathized with the embattled blacks. Golden's experience with race relations in Charlotte, North Carolina led him to believe that southern whites put great effort into "denying humanity to Negroes," by "depriving and dehumanizing" them because of their race.[1] As a result of his insight into southern race relations, he foresaw a revolution which he believed the major southern daily newspapers, generally owned by whites, would downplay because "to report this story meant describing the lot of the Negro."[2] Therefore, during the 1950s and 1960s Golden editorialized in favor of civil rights and racial equality through his newspaper, the *Carolina Israelite*. He also wrote numerous books,[3] wrote articles for other newspapers and magazines, and made personal and television/radio appearances. He utilized these outlets to foster better understanding and relations between black and white Americans. With the tools of his outspoken views and satiric humor, Golden wrote about the struggle for black civil rights by vividly illustrating the absurdity of racism and the ludicrous nature of segregationist traditions and policies.[4]

Golden's work had such an impact that Dr. Martin Luther King, Jr. identified Golden as one of four white journalists whom King believed were significant journalistic advocates in the fight for black civil rights. In essence, King considered Golden one of a small select group of white journalists who had "...grasped the meaning of this social revolution and committed themselves to it."[5] Dr. King also noted that Golden had "...recognized the urgency of the movement and sensed the need for powerful action, antidotes to combat the disease of segregation."[6]

Dr. King once termed the racial conflict in America as "a struggle between the forces of good and evil."[7] Harry Golden, a champion of civil rights, urged the deliverance of black Americans from the evil of racism and the wrong of segregation. His humorous style of advocacy was based on serious themes and motives. The liveliness of Golden's style of advocacy exemplified the zeal with which some segments of the press (national press, black press) not only covered but facilitated the civil rights movement.

Despite Golden's former celebrity and importance to the civil rights movement, he has been forgotten in contemporary accounts of the movement. Therefore, this book provides an historical examination of Golden and his advocacy. The book explores why and how Golden advocated civil rights for black Americans. In addition, the book addresses the significance of Golden's advocacy.

This book will 1) refresh the memories of former Golden fans and 2) introduce new generations to Golden. Younger readers, and those who are not familiar with the civil rights movement, will find Appendix A quite helpful. It provides an overview of the movement and the historical setting in which Golden lived and worked. Appendix B briefly highlights selected contemporaries of Golden who also used journalism to advocate racial equality.

Preface Notes

[1]Harry Golden, *The Right Time: An Autobiography, by Harry Golden* (New York: Putnam, 1969) 239.

[2]Golden, *The Right Time* 250.

[3]Harry Golden's books include: *The Best of Harry Golden* (Cleveland: World, 1967); *Carl Sandburg* (Cleveland: World, 1961); *Enjoy! Enjoy!* (Cleveland: World, 1960); *Ess, Ess Mein Kindt* (New York: Putnam, 1966); *For 2 Cents Plain* (Cleveland: World, 1958); *Forgotten Pioneer* (Cleveland: World, 1963); *The Golden Book of Jewish Humor* (New York: Putnam, 1972); *The Greatest Jewish City in the World* (Garden City: Doubleday, 1972); *The Israelis* (New York: Putnam, 1971); *Jews in American History* (Charlotte: Martin, 1950); *A Little Girl is Dead* (Cleveland: World, 1965); *Mr. Kennedy and the Negroes* (Cleveland: World, 1964); *Long Live Columbus* (New York: Putnam, 1975); *Only in America* (Cleveland:

World, 1958); *Our Southern Landsman* (New York: Putnam, 1974); *The Right Time* (New York: Putnam, 1969); *So Long as You're Healthy* (New York: Putnam, 1970); *So What Else is New?* (New York: Putnam, 1964); *Travels Through Jewish America* (Garden City: Doubleday, 1973); and *You're Entitle'* (Cleveland: World, 1962).

[4]William Goldhurst, "My Father, Harry Golden" *Midstream* June/July 1969: 68, 73; William Goldhurst, personal interview, 27 Feb. 1989.

[5]In addition to Golden, the other journalists were Ralph McGill, Lillian Smith, and James Dabbs. See Martin Luther King, Jr., *Letter from Birmingham City Jail* (Birmingham: American Friends Service Committee, 1963) 11.

[6]King, *Letter from Birmingham City Jail* 11.

[7]Ralph David Abernathy, *And the Walls Came Tumbling Down* (New York: Harper and Row, 1989) 468.

Acknowledgements

This book was started and successfully completed because of the many blessings of God. Many people also assisted me.

First and foremost, I wish to thank my wife and personal librarian Shirley R. Thomas. Her hard work and long days made this long project a reality. I also wish to thank Claire and Candace.

Next, I am indebted to Drs. Kurt Kent and William Goldhurst (one of Golden's sons)--both of the University of Florida, for introducing me to the marvelous world of Harry Golden. I also wish to thank my mentor, Dr. F. Leslie Smith for his early belief in me.

I am thankful for the work of Delores Jenkins and the kindness of Priscilla West--both of the University of Florida library. I am also thankful for the help and professionalism of Robin Brabham and Randy Penninger--both of the University of North Carolina at Charlotte library.

Last but not least, many others deserve special thanks including: Dr. Roderick McDavis, the late Dr. George Pozzetta, Dr. John Wright, Dr. William McKeen, Dr. Ralph Lowenstein, Clay Hallock, Justice John Charles Thomas, Justice Leah Sears, Floretta V.S. Thomas, Estelle Thomas, Jerelene Corcoran, Carlton R. Robinson, Dorethea Robinson, Caroline Cox, and Charles Frazier.

CHAPTER ONE

THE AMERICAN DREAM: GOLDEN'S MOTIVATION

Harry Golden's celebrity and importance to the civil rights movement (see the Preface) were possible because he was able to live the American dream. He saw the dream as the "opportunity to enter open society, to go from class to class, from income to income, from place to place, from one level to another."[1] Golden believed that all Americans should have the opportunity to do so. He also believed that obstructions which prevented segments of the population--such as blacks--from realizing the dream were blemishes on American society. Therefore, Golden encouraged Americans to perpetuate the dream for all citizens.[2]

Golden's progress toward and through the process of achieving the American dream motivated him to be concerned for others. This process began with the immigration of his family to the United States.

Immigration and Childhood

Harry Golden was born Herschele Lewis Goldhirsch in 1903 to Lieb and Anna Goldhirsch of Mikulintsky, Galicia.[3] Golden's family, several members at a time, came to America between 1904 and 1905. Lieb Goldhirsch sought a better life for his family and opportunities that were not available to them in their home land. According to Golden, for Jews like his family, Mikulintsky was a cage without bars where they could not go into business, work as civil servants, or serve in the military at a rank higher than sergeant. Such limitations prompted the move of the family.[4]

Golden's father and older brother, Jacob, migrated first in order to work and save money for the passage of Golden, his mother, and two sisters, Clara and Matilda. Lieb worked as a Hebrew teacher and Jacob worked as a peddler. The two lived and worked in Canada, Chicago, and Minneapolis before they moved to New York City and sent for the remainder of the family.[5] Upon the arrival of the family at the Ellis Island immigration center, an official inadvertently spelled the family name Goldhurst instead of Goldhirsch.[6] The family kept the new last name.

The reunited Goldhurst family settled in a four room apartment of a crowded tenement on the predominantly Jewish lower east side of New York City. Golden found the accommodations harsh and drab. Only two windows admitted sunlight into the crowded dwelling. Golden shared a windowless area with his younger brother, Max, and his older brother, Jacob. In addition, the kitchen served as the dining room as well as the bedroom for his two sisters. The kitchen stove was used to heat the apartment. Golden's family also shared an outdoor toilet with other tenants.[7]

Despite the crowding and poverty of the lower east side, the Goldhurst family, like many of the Jewish immigrants of the area, sought to make the most of the potential for success in America. Golden remembered the massive armies of garment workers and peddlers of all sorts of items who filled the streets of the lower east side. Such people demonstrated the need and importance of work. In the Goldhurst household everyone worked and contributed to the support of the family. Golden's father, a licensed notary, performed marriages and continued teaching Hebrew. Golden's mother worked as a seamstress while Jacob continued peddling. Clara and Matilda had factory jobs.[8]

Golden's means of helping out the family, and his first job, was selling newspapers. This early involvement with newspapers planted a seed which would one day grow and bloom into a substantial journalism career. Between 1912 and 1917, he sold papers for varied and numerous publications. Among the Jewish papers sold by Golden were the *Jewish Daily Forward*, the *Varheit*, the *Tageblatt* and the *Tog*. He also sold a Chinese paper, *Sa Mongee*, in Chinatown. In addition, Golden sold several large dailies including the *New York Globe*, *Journal*, *Mail*, *Post*, *Sun*, *Telegram*, and *World.*[9]

Throughout his childhood, Golden also worked in various other jobs to help out at home. At different times he worked as an errand boy, a pretzel delivery boy, a clothing delivery boy, a messenger, a hat sizer, and a sheet music salesperson.[10] Although he worked, Golden also found time to enjoy and learn from movies, reading, and school. According to Golden, east side boys loved the movies and went regularly. He believed that westerns, in particular, taught immigrant boys traits such as heroism which they admired and wanted to emulate in order to be liked by other

Americans.[11] To Golden, early westerns such as "Bronco Billy," conferred American ideals of manhood--"speak the truth and shoot straight."[12]

Golden also loved reading and school. As a child he had a deep affection for books from the moment he learned to read. He would read entire shelves of books at the library and always carried a book with him on the trolley car and at lunch during work. Golden's interest in reading helped him complete public school and three years of college--night school--at the City College of New York while holding jobs.[13] His love of reading combined with one of his childhood jobs led to one of the most important developmental experiences of his young life.

After starting a job as a stock clerk for a wealthy furrier, Oscar H. Geiger, Golden and Geiger became friends based on their mutual interest in reading. The teenage Golden's love of reading prompted Geiger to invite him to join a literary club. Geiger's Round Table Literary Club was primarily composed of middle and upper class boys of various religions--Protestant, Catholic, Jewish--who had a keen interest in reading.[14]

Golden believed that Geiger ran the club of ten boys[15] like a college seminar. Geiger required the boys to read and discuss books, deliver lectures, and debate each other. The boys read and discussed the works of writers such as Shakespeare, Milton, and Cervantes for the club. Golden also read the works of blacks such as Booker T. Washington and W.E.B. Dubois on his own.[16] The relationship with Geiger and the interaction with the Round Table Literary Club enabled Golden to enlarge his sphere of reading and to develop the critical thinking he would later call upon as a journalist and a social commentator.

Young Adulthood and Prison

Like his childhood job and association with Geiger, a job during Golden's young adulthood also had a great influence on his future journalism career. By the age of 23, a newly married Golden[17] had progressed from his series of childhood jobs to a stable position working at his sister Clara's stock and brokerage firm. After thoroughly learning the business during the mid-1920s, he decided to start a stock brokerage firm of his own--Kable and Company.[18]

Golden's firm specialized in the sale of stocks and bonds on a partial payment installment plan. Under this installment plan he promised customers that they could buy stocks and bonds at prevailing market prices. However, the stocks and bonds would not be transferred into the name of the customer until the full price had been paid. In addition, Golden collected his full commission from the first payment. Through the installment plan, he gained financial success. Whenever he made a profit for one investor, his friends, relatives, and neighbors would give him their money to invest.[19]

The confidence gained by Golden's success led him to venture into another variation of the partial payment plan called "bucketing", which held the potential for making more money quicker. Through bucketing a brokerage did not buy or sell stocks on the day the customer instructed the brokerage to do so. In essence, the firm waited for a stock to rise or fall and then would buy or sell the stock. Such late buying and selling allowed brokers to make an extra profit--beyond commissions--depending on how low the value of a stock went on a "buy order" or how high the value went on a "sell order" before the actual buy or sell.

If a broker waited too long to buy or sell he stood the chance of suffering great financial loss.[20]

Although Golden initially made money through bucketing, by 1926 he misjudged the stock market and waited too long to buy a stock which was on the way up in price. As a result, he lost money for himself and many of his customers. Golden could not afford to pay profits or repay the original investments to his investors. Consequently, he sold his house and declared bankruptcy. Based on the complaints of his upset customers, Golden was eventually indicted by a grand jury, tried, and convicted of using the mails to defraud. He had written to clients that they had credit balances with his brokerage when in fact neither the firm nor Golden had the funds to secure the claims.[21]

In 1929, Golden was sent to prison. He was determined to make the most of a bad situation and, therefore, made constructive use of his time. While in prison he served as a reading and mathematics teacher for other convicts. He also worked as a bookkeeper and a librarian. Highly significant, in terms of Golden's future journalism career, is the fact that he also had his first opportunity to work as a journalist. He served as the editor of the prison paper.[22]

At this point in Golden's life, he reached a crossroads. He decided that upon his release from prison he was going to get a fresh start and make the best of the remainder of his life. He did not want to suffer the consequences of any more ambitious business ventures such as the one which landed him in prison. Golden decided that he was going to take advantage of the knowledge he gained from years of reading and the experience he gained working on the prison paper by becoming a professional journalist.[23]

Freedom and Journalism

Golden was released from prison in 1933. With time off for good behavior he served almost four years--three years, eight months, and twenty-two days--of a five year sentence. His brother Jacob eased his transition back into free society by providing him with a job as a hotel manager in New York City. Golden took the job on the condition that he could resign at a moment's notice, pending success in his quest for a newspaper job. However, he was not initially successful in his search for a newspaper job and, therefore, worked at the hotel for five years.[24]

Like Golden's childhood job with Oscar Geiger, and his young adulthood job at Kable and Company, his hotel job was also significant in terms of the journalistic civil rights advocate he would become. Golden credited an incident which occurred during his years at the hotel as his "initiation into the civil right movement."[25] When Jack Johnson, the first black world heavyweight boxing champion, needed a hotel while staying in New York, Golden rented a room to Johnson despite the opposition of several white hotel guests. Golden wanted to do something because he was upset over the reaction of the white guests and sorry for Johnson.[26]

By 1938, Golden's ambition of becoming a professional journalist was well on the way to realization. He managed to get a job writing and selling promotional advertising for the *New York Mirror*. Golden went on to become a reporter for the *New York Post*. When the prospect of a higher paying job availed itself, Golden decided to leave New York and relocate to Norfolk, Virginia. He accepted a position as a promotional salesman with the *Norfolk Times-Advocate* where he sold space and wrote copy for advertisements. At this point in his career, Golden decided to change his last name from Goldhurst to Golden in order to disassociate his stock market and prison past from his new and promising journalism career.[27]

In 1941, Golden received a job offer to write editorials and sell advertising space for a North Carolina paper, the *Charlotte Labor Journal*--the official paper of the American Federation of Labor in North Carolina. With Golden's acceptance of the *Labor Journal* job, he headed for Charlotte. Several months after his arrival in Charlotte he changed jobs again. This time he was offered a position as an advertising salesman with the *Charlotte Observer*.[28] Golden's search for the best job had finally placed him in the right location to fulfill his destiny as an outspoken journalistic civil rights advocate.

Black Awareness and Advocacy

Golden's arrival in North Carolina made him highly aware of the desperate plight of blacks in the South. Likewise, his awareness led to the crystallization of his motivation to fight for black civil rights as well as his philosophical outlook on civil rights and race relations--racism, segregation--in the United States. When Golden first arrived in Charlotte, as a 39 year old northern Jew, he was admittedly "naive" in terms of personal experience with the severity of racism and segregation in the South.[29]

As a child on the lower east side, Golden rarely saw blacks, although he had read about them. Blacks were such a novelty that the first time he and his childhood friends saw a black man in their neighborhood they followed and watched him out of curiosity.[30] As a young adult, Golden rarely thought about the plight of blacks. He contended that as an immigrant Jew, he was "in haste" to adapt himself to the customs and traditions of his new country. In essence, he was busy attempting to become successful in business and a part of the society.[31]

Golden's naivete was soon replaced by the reality of southern race relations. After he settled in Charlotte, he came to believe that southern whites worked hard to deny "humanity to Negroes," by " depriving and dehumanizing" them because of their race.[32] For example, he revealed that as a white stranger to Charlotte and an immigrant in America, he would go for a walk and "Negroes whose ancestors had been in America for over three hundred years would step off the sidewalk and tip their hats" in deference to him.[33] When Golden attempted to sit in the "colored" section of a segregated bus in Charlotte he was verbally abused by the white driver until the bus reached his stop. Golden argued that "a white man could not even give his seat to a pregnant Negro woman" without both of them being "ordered off the bus" by the driver.[34]

The prevalence of institutionalized segregation in the South "nagged" Golden. He believed that such segregation made him as a white man an involuntary accomplice in the repression of blacks.[35] He was "nagged" when he spoke to blacks and they addressed him as "boss." He was "nagged" when he was answered "Yessah, Yessah," by blacks.[36] Most of all, Golden felt, "It was nagging to realize that Negroes were afraid of me."[37] The condition of race relations in Charlotte left Golden "morally vexed for the first time" in his life.[38] The plight of blacks in the South left him outraged.[39]

As an immigrant, Golden loved his life and freedom in America. He was deeply offended by the role of second-class citizen which had been forced upon blacks.[40] He believed that such a second-class citizenship was "dead wrong" and contrary to the American dream of freedom, justice, and opportunity for all.[41] Therefore, Golden wanted to save his beloved country from the hypocrisy of the second-class citizenship which he believed inflicted cruelty upon blacks and corrupted whites.[42]

Golden's enlightenment on conditions in the South led him to develop a sense that the South was on the verge of a revolution. He foresaw a revolution--the civil rights movement--which he believed the southern white press would down play because reporting this story meant "describing the lot of the Negro" to the world.[43] Golden concluded that the story would one day be his.[44]

Jewry and Civil Rights

Golden was motivated by his outrage over the plight of blacks in the South. He was also motivated by his love for America and desire to make it better--rid it of a second-class citizenship--and his recognition of a void in the fair and accurate press coverage of blacks. In addition, Golden's Jewish heritage served as a factor which prompted him to advocate black civil rights. Golden's awareness of his ancestry contributed to his personal concern for the well-being of blacks. As a Jew, he empathized with the suffering and cruelty inflicted upon blacks by whites in the South. He was well aware of similar suffering endured by Jews throughout history. Golden believed that, were it not for the immigration of his family, they would have all perished in the holocaust during World War II.[45] His concern for the well being of others also stemmed from his mother's devout observance of Judaism.[46] According to

Golden, his mother's whole life was family and religion.[47] As a result of his mother's strict attendance at synagogue, Golden also attended regularly during his childhood and was instilled with a concern for his fellow man.[48]

Golden believed that the struggle for civil rights by blacks was directly related to Jews and that Jews as well as blacks would benefit from the fight. He believed, "when a man fights for others he fights for himself."[49] To Golden the civil rights movement caused the American Constitution to become a "living document" which protects the rights of all citizens, including Jews.[50] He also believed that the fight by blacks for their civil rights set an excellent example which Jews and others could follow.[51]

Although Golden's Jewish heritage was a motivating factor in his civil rights advocacy, such was not the case with the southern Jewish community as a whole. According to Golden, some southern Jews took a less active part in the struggle for black civil rights.[52] He believed that such Jews were nervous when it came to civil rights and they did not want to "rock the boat."[53] Golden thought that some Jews would rather maintain "strict neutrality" than run the risk of replacing blacks as "scapegoats"--victims--in the southern white gentile society.[54] (Golden's thoughts on southern Jews and the civil rights movement are also supported by others writing on the topic such as Lenwood Davis and Leonard Dinnerstein.[55])

Golden also believed that some southern Jews went beyond neutrality to hostility toward blacks. In one such instance, Golden used the *Carolina Israelite* to respond to a fellow Jew who was upset about black demands for civil rights. The man thought that blacks, unlike Jews, Italians, Greeks, and others, failed to pull themselves up by their bootstraps.[56] In his editorial response to what he termed "A Letter from an Angry Jew" Golden argued that Jews,

Italians, Greeks, and others could not have pulled themselves up if they had to face racism and segregation from the majority of the American population when attempting to better themselves. Golden stressed that blacks faced race related obstacles that were imposed on them by the larger society. According to Golden:

> We Jews would not have pulled ourselves up by our bootstraps if we had to sit in the back of the bus and if we could not enter a restaurant and if every conceivable obstacle were thrown in the way of our voting and our schooling.[57]

Golden's Civil Rights Philosophy

Golden derived motivation to fight for black civil rights from various life circumstances and his Jewish heritage. Similarly, the factors which motivated Golden also led him to develop his own outlook on civil rights advocacy. For example, Golden's awareness of a lack of support for the civil rights movement by southern Jews led him to develop his "Es vet Gurnisht Helffren" or "nothing helps" philosophy of Jewish participation in the civil rights movement.[58] Based on this philosophy, Golden believed that southern white gentiles routinely accused the Jews of instigating blacks to demand civil rights. As a result, Golden saw the neutrality of southern Jews as futile in terms of minimizing the accusations. Therefore, he reasoned that southern Jews might as well help out with the civil rights movement because they were going to be blamed anyway.[59]

Golden's philosophy on the need for a civil rights movement stemmed from his belief that the flaw of racism in American society resulted in the unfair and unequal treatment of blacks. Golden believed that such unfairness and inequality was manifested through problems including not only segregation, but the denial of voting rights, substandard health care, and inadequate educational and employment opportunities for blacks.[60] Golden was disturbed by what he perceived as irony in the unfair and unequal treatment of blacks by whites.

For example, on the issue of segregation, Golden wondered how and why blacks were allowed to provide service to whites in the best hotels yet could not sleep there themselves.[61] In terms of the denial of black voting rights, he wondered how whites could allow blacks to supervise the affairs of their [white] households and care for their children, yet, place "a million obstacles in his [blacks] path when he wants to vote."[62] On the issue of health care, Golden wondered "why in these great rich United States [in 1960], the infant mortality rate of the Negro is five times that of whites?"[63] In terms of education and employment, he wondered why he saw so few black physicians and other professionals and such an abundance of black waiters, maids, and janitors.[64] Golden knew that this irony was nonetheless reality for black Americans.

Golden also believed that the plight of blacks was related to another manifestation of racism, namely caste. According to Golden, southern whites felt that "the Negro stood between them [southern whites] and social oblivion."[65] He contended that poor whites, in particular, needed to have blacks in a subservient position in order to maintain their own self esteem and prevent the diminishment of their status as whites.[66]

Golden maintained that the advancement of blacks through the American caste system was necessary for the well being of blacks as well as whites. He thought that black progress into the "mainstream of American society"[67] would bring even greater victories to white southerners. Golden believed that when you "draw a line" and say that "certain people should not cross it," you will spend the rest of your life "watching the line."[68] In this regard, Golden also believed that southern whites would one day have to stop watching the "other side of the line" or the "back of the bus" which would result in the freedom to continue on with their own lives.[69]

Golden also saw the fight for civil rights in a broader context. He acknowledged the idea that blacks, because of color, could not simply change their names and identities as other groups had done to hide their origins. Therefore, blacks had to fight for laws to counteract the manifestations of racism.[70] However, Golden felt that even though blacks were identified with the need for civil rights, the fight for civil rights was one for all Americans.[71]

Chapter One Notes

[1]Harry Golden, "The American Dream," *Johns Hopkins Magazine* April 1962: 36.

[2]Golden, "The American Dream," 8, 36-37.

[3]Mikulintsky, Galicia was formerly a part of the Soviet Union; William Goldhurst, personal interview, 27 Feb. 1989; Harry Golden, *The Right Time: An Autobiography, by Harry Golden* (New York: Putnam, 1969) 19; Harry Golden, letter to Tom Davis, 30 Sept. 1968, Box 9 File 10, Harry Golden Collection Part II, U of North Carolina at Charlotte.

[4]Golden, *The Right Time* 19.

[5]Harry Golden, "1910's: Harry Golden," *Five Boyhoods*

ed. Martin Levin (New York: Doubleday, 1962) 45; Golden, *The Right Time* 20.

[6]Golden, "1910's" 44; Golden, *The Right Time* 19, 20, 28; Harry Golden, *Travels through Jewish America* (Garden City: Doubleday, 1973) 1; Golden used the last name Goldhurst until he began his career as a professional journalist. See "Professional Development" section of this chapter.

[7]Golden, *The Right Time* 21-22; Golden, *Travels through Jewish America* 2; Harry Golden, "Five Boyhoods," *Carolina Israelite* May-June 1962: 11; Golden, "1910's" 39, 41; According to Golden, the address of the Goldhurst family was 171 Eldridge Street.

[8]Golden, "1910's" 50, 51, 55; Golden, *Travels through Jewish America* 2; Harry Golden, foreword, *A Bintel Brief* by Isaac Metzker (New York: Ballantine, 1971) 13-30.

[9]Golden, *The Right Time* 54; Golden, "1910's" 61, 63; Irving Howe, "The Yiddish Press," *World of Our Fathers* (New York: Simon and Schuster, 1976) 520, 523, 533, 545.

[10]Golden, "1910's" 61, 71; Golden, *The Right Time* 55-58.

[11]Golden, "1910's" 67; Irving Howe "Growing Up in the Ghetto," *World of Our Fathers* (New York: Simon and Schuster, 1976) 259.

[12]Golden, "1910's" 67.

[13]Golden, "1910's" 54, 60, 61; Golden, *The Right Time* 45, 53.

[14]Golden, "1910's" 72-73.

[15]In addition to Golden, the other members of the Round Table Literary Club included: George Geiger, Oscar Geiger's son; John Duff, Golden's closest friend in the club; Murray DeLeeuw; Milton Bergerman; Sidney Davidson; Robert Gomperts; Chester Edelman; Henry Lowenberg; Elliott Barrett; and Milton Norwalk. See Golden, *The Right Time* 66.

[16]Golden, "1910's" 74-75; Golden, *The Right Time* 66-67.

[17]Golden married Genevieve Alice Marie Gallagher "Tiny" in 1926. She was an Irish Catholic school teacher from

Scranton, Pennsylvania. The couple had four children: Richard, a writer who also served as Golden's associate editor at the *Israelite*; Harry Jr.--now deceased--a reporter who worked at various times for the *Charlotte Observer*, the *Detroit Free Press*, the *New York Post*, and the *Chicago Sun-Times*; William, a writer and professor of American Literature at the University of Florida; and Peter, who was born mentally retarded and institutionalized until he died at the age of 19. Source: William Goldhurst, personal interview, 27 Feb. 1989; Golden, *The Right Time* 97, 216-217.

[18]Robert Honner, "The Other Harry Golden: Harry Goldhurst and the Cannon Scandals." *The North Carolina Historical Review* 65 (1988): 155; Golden went into business with a nominal partner, Charles Kable, in order to use Kable's name for the company. Golden did not want to use the Goldhurst name so that he could prevent encroachment on Clara's firm, C. Goldhurst Company. See Golden, *The Right Time* 114.

[19]Golden, *The Right Time* 115.

[20]Golden, *The Right Time* 117.

[21]Honner, 165; Golden, *The Right Time* 120. The 1929 case of *United States v. Goldhurst and Kable* was not recorded in a legal reporter.

[22]Golden, *The Right Time* 154-155.

[23]Harry Golden, *For 2 Cents Plain* (Cleveland World, 1958) 20; Golden, *The Right Time* 154-155, 210.

[24]Golden, *The Right Time* 163, 171-173; Honner, 171. In 1973, after Golden had gained fame as a journalist, President Richard Nixon, at the request of Golden, granted Golden executive clemency for his mail fraud conviction; see Kays Gary, "Golden Pardoned for 1929 Crime" *The Charlotte Observer* 7 Dec. 1973; 1a-2a.

[25]Golden, *The Right Time* 180.

[26]Harry Golden, *The Best of Harry Golden* (Cleveland: World, 1967) 352; Golden, *The Right Time* 180.

[27]Harry Golden, *Harry Golden on Various Matters* (New York: Anti Defamation League of B'nai B'rith, 1966) 5; Golden, *The Right Time* 224.

[28]Golden, *The Right Time* 201, 224, 226, 250.

[29]Golden, *The Right Time* 238.

[30]Golden, "1910's" 64.

[31]Golden, *The Right Time* 116.

[32]Golden, *The Right Time* 239.

[33]Golden, *The Right Time* 237.

[34]Golden, *The Right Time* 238.

[35]Golden, *The Right Time* 242.

[36]Golden, *The Right Time* 242.

[37]Golden, *The Right Time* 242.

[38]Golden, *The Right Time* 242.

[39]Harry Golden, interview, *Sunday Morning*. CBS TV 25 October 1981; Harry Golden, "Civil Rights for a Selfish Reason," *Carolina Israelite* April 1964: 9; Arnold Markowitz, "Sense of Outrage Still Golden," *Miami Herald* 12 March 1972: 6N; William Goldhurst, personal interview, 30 March 1990.

[40]William Goldhurst, personal interview, 30 March 1990.

[41]Golden, *Sunday Morning*.

[42]Golden, *The Right Time* 239.

[43]Golden, *The Right Time* 250; Golden, *Sunday Morning*.

[44]Golden, *Sunday Morning*; William Goldhurst personal interview, 30 Jan. 1990; See Chapter 2 for a discussion of Golden's journalistic civil rights advocacy.

[45]Golden, *Sunday Morning*.

[46]Golden, "1910's" 57.

[47]Golden, "1910's" 58.

[48]Golden, "1910's" 43.

[49]Golden, *Harry Golden on Various Matters* 47.

[50]Harry Golden, "Harry Golden," *Negro and Jew: An Encounter in America* ed. Shlomo Katz (New York: Macmillan, 1967) 64.

[51]Golden, *Harry Golden on Various Matters* 47.

[52]Golden, *Harry Golden on Various Matters* 31. According to Golden and others, with the exception of several southern rabbis, such as Abraham Heschel, Perry Nussbaum, Alfred Goodman, Charles Martinband, and Jacob Rothchild most southern Jews kept silent on the issue of segregation; see Harry Golden, "Integration and the Jews," *Carolina Israelite* March-April 1960: 7; Allen Krause, "The Southern Rabbi and Civil Rights," thesis, Hebrew Union College, 1967, 142, 184, 136, 238; Juan Williams, *Eyes on the Prize: America's Civil Rights Years, 1954-65* (New York: Penguin, 1988) 279; and Lenwood G. Davis, *Black-Jewish Relations in the United States, 1752-1984* (Westport: Greenwood, 1984) xii; Charles Mantiband, letters to Harry Golden, 2 April 1960, 4 May 1963, and 1 Sept. 1963, Box 13 File 7, Harry Golden Collection Part II, U of North Carolina, Charlotte; Harry Golden, letter to Charles Mantiband, 8 April 1960, Box 13 File 7, Harry Golden Collection Part II, U of North Carolina, Charlotte.

[53]Harry Golden, "Jew and Gentile in the New South," *Commentary* Nov. 1955: 412.

[54]Golden, "Jew and Gentile" 412; Golden, "Integration and the Jews" 7.

[55]See Davis xi-xiii; Leonard Dinnerstein, "Southern Jewry and the Desegregation Crisis, 1954-1970," *American Jewish Historical Quarterly* 62 (1973): 231; Gus Solomon, *The Jewish Role in the American Civil Rights Movement* (London: Jewish World Congress, 1967) 22; and Ben Halpern, *Jews and Blacks* (New York: Herder and Herder, 1971) 182; Davis, Dinnerstein, and other scholars also contend that many northern Jews did actively support and participate in the fight for black civil rights. For example, northern Jews were among the founders of the NAACP and CORE. In addition, northern Jews worked for and with other civil rights groups such as SCLC and SNCC.

[56]Harry Golden, "Letter to an Angry Jew," *Carolina Israelite* Sept.-Oct. 1960: 17.

[57]Golden, "Letter to" 17.

[58]Golden, "Harry Golden on Various Matters" 33; Golden, "Integration and the Jews" 7.

[59]Golden, "Harry Golden on Various Matters" 33.

[60]Golden, *For 2 Cents Plain* 251; Golden, *The Right Time* 246; Golden, "The American Dream" 8.

[61]Golden, *For 2 Cents Plain* 251.

[62]Golden, *For 2 Cents Plain* 251.

[63]Golden, "The American Dream" 8.

[64]Golden, *The Right Time* 246.

[65]Golden, "Harry Golden on Various Matters" 31-32.

[66]Golden, "Harry Golden on Various Matters" 32; Golden, "The American Dream" 36.

[67]Golden, "Harry Golden on Various Matters" 20.

[68]Harry Golden, "The Negroes Give Us a Free Ride," *Carolina Israelite* Jul.-Aug. 1966: 14; Golden, "Harry Golden on Various Matters" 32.

[69]Golden, "The Negroes Give" 14.

[70]Harry Golden, *So Long As You're Healthy* (New York: Putnam, 1970) 128-129; Harry Golden, *Ess, Ess Mein Kindt* (New York: Putnam, 1966) 318.

[71]Golden, *Ess, Ess Mein Kindt* 212-213.

CHAPTER TWO

THE GOLDEN WAY: GOLDEN'S METHOD

The Carolina Israelite

Harry Golden started his own newspaper, the *Carolina Israelite*, on a trial basis while working for the *Charlotte Observer*. According to Golden, the *Israelite* was first produced in October of 1941 as a sample publication and 800 free copies were mailed out.[1] The first several years of the *Israelite* were dedicated to coverage of the Jewish community. However, during the 1950s and 1960s he focused the paper extensively on civil rights advocacy.[2]

During the 1940s, the paper's prime liberal stance was Jewish-Christian brotherhood and understanding.[3] The paper covered topics such as anti-semitism, Jewish contributions to American society, Jews in World War II, Jews in medicine and science, the holocaust, and the history of Jews in the United States.[4] In addition, the paper's banner at one time included the phrase "A Monthly Review of Jewish Affairs, Dedicated to Interfaith Amity" after the name.[5]

As Golden became more aware of and sensitive to the plight of blacks in Charlotte and throughout the South,[6] he decided to become an advocate of civil rights for blacks. He believed that blacks were capable of fighting their own fight, but he felt compelled to help in his own way.[7] Golden's way was through switching from the printing of "news," personal and social columns, press releases, and wire service coverage.[8] His own way was through shifting to the editorialization and advocacy of personal journalism[9] in order to reflect his perceptions of and sensitivity to the black struggle for civil rights.[10] He wanted to use the *Israelite* to point out how racism and segregation had harmed blacks and degraded whites.[11]

Golden's way was not through targeting the *Israelite* at a black audience, although he kept in close contact with the black community.[12] Instead, Golden decided to aim the paper at white liberals because he believed they could and would provide supplementary support for the movement by working for the advancement of blacks.[13] Therefore, he sought to "recruit Jews and gentiles into the movement for civil rights for colored citizens" through the use of the *Carolina Israelite*.[14] In order to accomplish his objective of civil rights advocacy and social commentary through the *Israelite*, Golden decided to emulate the personal journal and personal journalism of a friend, Emanuel Haldeman-Julius. Between 1916 and 1951, Haldeman-Julius published the *American Freeman*, a personal journal, as well as numerous other publications in Girard, Kansas.[15]

Like Golden, Haldeman-Julius came from a family of Jewish immigrants, loved reading, and worked throughout his youth to help support his family.[16] Also like Golden,

Haldeman-Julius was described as a philosopher, humorist, editorialist, and objective thinker.[17] This commonality not only led to friendship but to mutual admiration.[18] Golden considered Haldeman-Julius a model personal journalist.[19] Haldeman-Julius considered Golden a "good writer" with a "lively, bright, and reasonable style" who was an excellent source on the South.[20]

Golden was influenced by the frank opinionated writing of Haldeman-Julius and the format and style of the *American Freeman*.[21] He considered the *Freeman* "the prototype of the *Israelite*."[22] Likewise, Haldeman-Julius took credit for Golden's personal journalism in the *Israelite*. He noted, "It is my guess that my behavior as a writer has influenced him [Golden]."[23] The *Freeman*, like the *Israelite*, primarily ran editorials and social commentary. Topic coverage included food, literature, politics, religion, science, and autobiographical sketches by Haldeman-Julius.[24] Haldeman-Julius used the *Freeman* as a sounding board to address whatever issues he felt needed comment. According to Haldeman-Julius, "My pen is always used to write what I really feel and not what expediency might say I should put into words."[25] Golden sought to harness the same idealism in attacking racism and advocating civil rights for blacks. Although the *Freeman* was not used for civil rights advocacy, as was the *Israelite*, Haldeman-Julius, like Golden was a foe of racism. He considered racial prejudice a significant societal problem and sympathized with blacks.[26] According to Haldeman-Julius, prejudice and injustice distorted white perceptions of blacks. Haldeman-Julius also believed that discrimination was indefensible and that blacks should be treated as fellow human beings by whites. He noted that until blacks, like whites, were judged based on individual personality and behavior, there would be problems in race relations.[27]

Haldeman-Julius's intolerance of racism is exemplified by his reaction to the treatment of blacks in public facilities. He took offense during a concert by black opera star Marian Anderson when he noticed that 75 blacks, out of an audience of 3,000 whites, were "shunted into a remote corner of the concert hall [the right side of the balcony]."[28] In addition, he complained that Anderson could not get a hotel room or eat at a "decent" restaurant while in Joplin, Missouri for her concert. Haldeman-Julius was also upset by the lack of depth exhibited by the local paper in interviewing Anderson after the concert. He revealed:

> All this reporter could bring up in the presence of a superb artist was a series of questions about her hobbies--Did she make her own dress?, Was she interested in house work?, Did she cook?[29]

Haldeman-Julius, like Golden, was against racism. As mentioned earlier, the *Freeman* was not used for civil rights advocacy. Instead, Golden saw the *Freeman* as a prototype and sought to emulate the style and format of the *Freeman* in the pages of the *Israelite.* Golden wanted to capture the essence of the frank, opinionated writing used by Haldeman-Julius. However, Golden's brand of frank, opinionated writing had an added dimension--humor.

Serious Humor and Golden Plans

Golden was a humorous, personable, and caring man who used frank, satiric humor as a tool to facilitate better interracial communication, understanding, and acceptance. He pointed out injustice in a humorous way[30] because he felt that people had "little sympathy with stolidity."[31] He believed that the use of humor increased the likelihood that people would pay attention to and accept his point of view.[32]

Golden's use of satiric humor stemmed from his Jewish heritage. He considered humor "a part of the Jewish culture."[33] According to Golden, Jewish humor was a "deeply pessimistic irony" born of a need to mitigate centuries of "despair, poverty, and terror in Europe."[34] In essence, to Golden Jewish humor was a defense against a "hostile society."[35]

Golden believed "the more desperate the problem the more humor was needed."[36] He also believed that the hopes of blacks and Jews for equality and acceptance by the white gentile American society was equally intense.[37] As a result, Golden used the tradition of Jewish humor in his advocacy of civil rights for blacks. In the process, he clothed much of his criticism of racism and segregation in satire.[38]

The Golden Plans

Throughout the pages of the *Israelite*, Golden attempted to promote laughter among his readership as a bridge of communication and understanding. He used his satiric wit to stimulate the public scrutiny of racist beliefs, traditions, and policies. Prevalent in the *Israelite*, between 1956 and 1968, was a series of 17 seemingly ridiculous recommendations for resolving various race related problems. These "Golden Plans" illustrate Golden's satiric humor and stance on racism and segregation.

The Vertical Negro Plan. Golden was prompted to write this, his first, plan in response to southern resistance to the

Supreme Court's *Brown v. Board of Education* decision.[39] He asserted that the North Carolina state legislature was considering legislation which would eliminate the state's compulsory school attendance law in order to prevent integration. He also noted that such legislation would establish educational expense grants in order to promote the establishment of private schools. In addition, Golden contended that the legislation would provide a local option whereby the majority of people in a school district--usually white--could elect to close any school.[40]

As a result of such resistance, Golden proposed a plan to prevent the elimination of the public system of education and save "millions of dollars" in school duplication costs. He commented that in the South, "vertical segregation" had been eliminated. According to Golden, "Whites and Negroes" stood at the same supermarket counter; deposited money at the same teller's window; walked through the same department stores; and stood at the same drugstore counters without incident.[41] Therefore, he suggested that all seats be taken out of public schools and replaced with standing desks. He stressed that the plan would allow white and black students to stand and learn together.[42]

Four years after Golden's 1956 introduction of this plan for school children, he adapted it for a slightly different use. He noted that the University of Alabama offered televised college courses for which only whites could receive credit--a picture or written declaration of race was required on each application. Therefore, based on the Vertical Negro Plan, Golden offered a solution for blacks who wanted credit for the televised courses. He suggested that they promise on their application to stand up during the airing of all televised courses offered by the University.[43]

The Out-of-Order Plan. In response to segregation of public facilities, Golden suggested a way to integrate and eliminate the cost of duplication. He concluded that due to tradition and intimidation, blacks were reluctant to use "white only" water fountains. However, Golden believed that whites would use "colored only" water fountains if no other option existed. Therefore, he suggested that an out-of-order sign be placed on "white only" water fountains. He theorized that whites would use the "colored only" fountains. He also believed that the plan could easily be extended to rest rooms.[44]

The White Baby Plan. Responding to segregation at entertainment outlets--plays, concerts--Golden noted that blacks who served as care givers--baby sitters, maids--for white children routinely gained access to white theaters without hesitation when accompanying a white child. Therefore, Golden recommended that blacks who desired to attend segregated plays and concerts should borrow a white child to take with them on such outings. Golden argued that the plan would also solve the baby-sitting problem of thousands of white working mothers. He also recommended that blacks eventually set up a factory and manufacture white babies made of plastic, thereby allowing them to go to an opera or a concert whenever they wanted to go. He added that the dolls should all have blond hair and blue eyes. Such dolls, according to Golden, would give blacks priority over whites for the best seats in the house.[45]

The Carry-the-Books Plan. In response to the "Little Rock Nine" school desegregation crisis in Little Rock, Arkansas,[46] Golden suggested a means through which black and white students could attend school together in peace. Noting that southern whites did not object to the presence of blacks who were servants or domestic workers, he proposed that black male students carry the books of their white male classmates, and black girls wear a miniature apron, like a maid, over their dresses. According to Golden, such a sacrifice by blacks would cause the mobs of segregationists to disband, thus eliminating the need for National Guard or federal troops.[47]

The Turban Plan. In response to the problems of racial segregation in hotels, restaurants, and other public places, Golden recommended a solution. He noted that southern whites accepted some foreigners more readily than they accepted blacks. He also contended that since the turban and the sari represented exotic and far away places, anyone wearing one or the other could easily go to a movie, ride a bus, or get a hotel room without fear of rejection. Therefore, Golden suggested that black men wear turbans and black women wear saris in order to pass themselves off as Egyptians, Arabs, Indians, or other foreigners. He asserted that the use of such clothing would not only end racial segregation, but would bring much needed money to the North Carolina textile industry.[48]

The White Citizens Plan. Through this plan Golden commented on the loss of popularity of the White Citizens Councils.[49] He noted that the loss of popularity was partially based on the fact that most major Christian religious denominations in the South, "the backbone of the citizens councils," decided to back integration after the *Brown v. Board of Education* Supreme Court decision.[50] Golden believed that various large white Christian religious denominations would themselves become integrated next. Therefore, he suggested that the white gentile members of the citizens council who really wanted to get away from blacks should "become Jews." As Jews, he noted, they would have "their own country clubs, swimming pools, rummage sales, and book reviews." In addition, they would "never have to worry about Negroes again."[51]

The Standing Room Only Plan. In response to segregated movie houses, Golden noted that southern whites did not mind standing with blacks. Therefore, he proposed another adaptation of his Vertical Negro Plan. In this case he recommended that movie house owners remove all seats from their theaters and place "Standing Room Only" signs in front of the buildings. He reasoned that standing through a two hour movie would not be comfortable. As a result, he also recommended that "Vertical Hammocks" be installed so that patrons could lean during the movie. According to Golden, this plan would give blacks a chance to finally see first-run movies like whites. He also noted that the plan would revive movie attendance by making all patrons believe that the movies were very popular because the term "standing room only" usually indicated all seats were in use.[52]

The Pogo Stick Plan. Through this plan Golden offered an additional adaptation of the Vertical Negro Plan as a solution for striking white Detroit, Michigan police officers. The white officers refused to issue traffic tickets as a show of outrage for having to ride--sit--in patrol cars with black officers. Golden noted that for many years white and black police officers had walked their beats peacefully. Therefore, he suggested that the Detroit police force should use pogo sticks instead of patrol cars as a means of transportation. According to Golden, such a situation would allow the white officers to work with black officers in a vertical position. He concluded, "After all, they cannot patrol the whole city on foot."[53]

The Loud-Talk Consensus Plan. Golden argued that segregation and the poor treatment of black by whites was based on fear fostered by myths and stereotypes. However, he also asserted that on a race-to-race basis whites were not usually discourteous to blacks. Along these lines, Golden recalled an incident where a black man attempted to eat at a small segregated restaurant in the South. The man was politely informed by a white waitress that he could not be served because the white diners would leave if he was. Upon the refusal of service the black man stood up, clapped his hands to gain the attention of the white customers, and announced aloud that he wanted to eat but would leave if anyone objected. When no one objected the man was served breakfast. Golden suggested that similar action by blacks around the country might end racial segregation by consensus.[54]

The Save-the-Quiz-Show Plan. Through this plan, Golden responded to the voter qualification test that blacks were required to take in order to vote in the South. He noted that television game shows might be made more interesting and lively by asking contestants questions similar to those used on the voter tests, such as "How many bubbles are in a pound of soap?"[55] According to Golden, white voter registration officials from the South should be used as contestants. He asserted that such a solution would not only perk up the game show ratings, but publicize the futility of taking such tests.[56]

The Color-Happy Semi-Darkness Plan. When a white child with a dark complexion was mistaken for a light skinned black and consequently chased out of her North Carolina school, Golden took aim at "color insanity" in the South. First, he suggested that in order to prevent a similar situation from recurring, all southern school boards should "make provisions for children who have been tanned by the sun as well as those who are naturally dark.[57] He went on to recommend different classes for each different shade. For example, "peaches and cream complexions in one room" and "milk white" in another.[58]

According to Golden, such a system of classes based on complexion would provide work for a battery of Color experts who would be responsible for determining exact skin shade. However, Golden warned that children might have to be reassigned room to room as their color changed with the seasons. He also warned that families exhibiting a range of skin shades might be forcibly separated.[59]

In addition, Golden also suggested that lighting should be taken into consideration in determining room assignment. He noted that lighting had an "effect upon both complexion and illusion."[60] Therefore, Golden recommended that "the best solution would be to hold all classes in semi-darkened rooms."[61] According to Golden, "all the work would be done by memory and with phosphorescent chalk."[62] He warned racists that students might form friendships on the basis of personality, common concern, and interest, instead of skin color.[63]

The Dihydroxyactone Plan. According to Golden, a drug on the market, dihydroxyactone, could change white skin to brown. Therefore, he decided to discuss the potential benefit of the drug as a solution for racial problems. He noted that the drug could "kill two birds with one swallow"[64] by making everyone the same. As a result, he contended that dihydroxyactone could be used to put an end to the expense of dual, segregated, school systems and public facilities. Golden also asserted that the drug could put an end to the fears of whites who refused to work or associate with blacks. He remarked, "$3.40 a bottle" was a small amount to pay to put an end to segregation."[65]

The Bond Issue Plan. Through this plan Golden noted that Jackson, Mississippi and many other southern cities boasted about their total large population--a combination of white, black, and other race--when seeking a high municipal bond rating or attempting to lure new businesses and industry. He argued that such southern cities "want it both ways" because they want to "include Negroes as part of their population but exclude them as people."[66] He suggested that the black population figure be segregated on bond applications so as to reflect the fact that blacks were not really citizens, but a separate "less-equal-than-white" group of people.[67]

The No Rent Plan. Golden believed that white segregationists would experience "terrible anguish" upon the implementation of federal open housing legislation. Such legislation would prohibit racial discrimination in government financed housing. He also believed that blacks would attempt to gain access to government financed homes and apartments. As a result, Golden decided to comment on the potential opposition he thought blacks would face from their new white neighbors.

Golden indicated that prior to the proposed federal legislation, some blacks already lived in the finest homes and most modern apartments in the country. He also noted that these blacks were welcomed in their neighborhoods and did not have to pay rent or mortgages. The blacks Golden spoke of were "janitors, domestics, servants, and valets."[68] According to Golden, "only the Negro who wants to pay rent or mortgage is in trouble" and "denied" because he seeks equality.[69] He also noted that, "A Negro in a white jacket with a leather bow tie is acceptable any place."[70] Therefore, Golden proposed that blacks who wanted to move into the suburbs or white housing areas should wear "a white jacket and a bow tie for men" and "an apron for women."[71] He asserted that such outfits would quell opposition and satisfy the white neighbors. He also added "of course, the Negroes must pay no rent to be acceptable."[72]

The Potemkin Toilet Plan. Golden proposed an adaptation of his Out-of-Order Plan in response to racial segregation in public rest rooms. He noted that during many auditorium events there were usually more white women waiting in line to use the "white only" rest room than there were black women in line waiting to use the "colored only" rest room. He revealed that during the intermission of an event he attended "no fewer than 28 white ladies were waiting in line to get into the powder room" while "the powder room of the Negro women was empty and silent."[73] Therefore, he suggested that "white only" rest rooms be done away with at arenas and fake doors marked with "white only " and "temporarily out of order/use Negro door" signs be installed. According to Golden, the plan would desegregate and save money on duplication.[74]

The Alabama-Mississippi Plan. Golden used this plan to comment on separate-but-equal schools. He contended that Governors Ross Barnett of Mississippi and George Wallace of Alabama claimed that there was no reason to integrate public schools. According to Golden, both men argued that the black and white schools in their respective states were equal. Therefore, Golden suggested a test of the equality in Mississippi and Alabama. He recommended that black and white students exchange schools. Under this plan the white students would transfer to the "equal Negro schools" and the blacks would transfer to the "previous all white" schools. However, Golden added, the faculty, library, and other facilities were to remain in place at each of the "equal" schools.[75]

The Insurance Plan. Through this plan, Golden responded to the bombing of black homes and churches in Mississippi and Alabama. He noted that insurance companies in Mississippi and Alabama were underwriting new southern skyscrapers and shopping centers in addition to issuing accident and retirement plans for southern industry. He contended that the insurance companies were important businesses which were usually owned by influential southern white citizens. Therefore, Golden suggested that all Negroes and civil rights workers in the South take out a $25,000 term insurance policy before going to church, to vote, or on a trip throughout the South. He also proposed a "Golden Negro Insurance Fund" to pay the premiums. Noting that the insurance companies probably did not want to go broke, Golden theorized that the influential white owners of the companies would not sit idly by while their insured clients and buildings were being blown and shot up. He asserted that they would, consequently, "put an end to the terror, bombing, and killing."[76]

Use of the Plans

Although most of the Golden plans were offered in jest, several were taken seriously and a few were actually implemented. For example, the Vertical Negro Plan was used in several different places.[77] According to Golden, this plan was used in 1957 by a department store in High Point, North Carolina. At that time the store management had all of the stools taken out of the store's snack counter. Golden found humor in being taken seriously by the store. Although he had hopes that the stools would eventually come back--along with integration--Golden also saw several steps to the replacement of the stools. He commented, "Maybe one day Negroes can lean against the seats in a half-standing position" or "Maybe they will get to a forty-five degree angle without stirring up anything."[78]

Golden also indicated that the Vertical Plan was used at other places. According to Golden, in 1962 the Danville, Virginia public library "took all the tables and chairs out."[79] He noted that in 1962 the restaurant at the Jackson, Mississippi municipal airport "pulled all the chairs out" so everybody could "eat standing up."[80] He also noted that in 1963 the Albany, Georgia public library "took all the chairs out" and blacks and whites had to stand together.[81] In addition to the Vertical Negro Plan, Golden indicated that following the Turban Plan, a black newsman from Pittsburgh made a tour of the South wearing a turban. According to Golden, "the man was welcomed with open arms in the best hotels and a white women's society event sent him flowers and an invitation to make a speech."[82] Golden also indicated that a "Negro Literary Club" in North Carolina "adopted my suggestion to wear turbans."[83] The 80 members planned to "venture forth once a week to cafes, movies, or wherever they wanted to go."[84]

Golden's Out-of-Order Plan was also successfully used. He persuaded a North Carolina department store manager to implement the plan. According to Golden "for the first day or two the whites were hesitant, but little by little they began to drink out of the "colored only" fountain. He noted that by the end of three weeks, "everybody was drinking integrated water without a single complaint."[85]

Other Forms of Commentary

Golden used his Golden Plans to offer suggestions and recommendations for various racial problems. In addition, he also used satire through the *Israelite* in other ways, to comment on racial injustice. Golden utilized unique editorial forms--awards, poems, anecdotes--to respond to a variety of race-related themes.

For example, Golden announced a "Bull Connor Award" in the *Israelite* in order to comment on the harsh treatment of black civil rights demonstrators by the police and fire departments under the control of Birmingham, Alabama Public Safety Commissioner Eugene "Bull" Connor.[86] According to Golden, competition for the award would be open to all black and white Birmingham high school seniors. The award would include a college scholarship and a bronze medallion showing Connor directing police dogs. Golden also stressed that the medallion would be suspended by a piece of hose instead of the usual ribbon.[87]

Golden tried his hand at poetry on at least one occasion. In response to the jailing of civil rights sit-in demonstrators throughout the South he wrote: "Thirty days hath September, April June, and November And any Negro who tries to eat at Howard Johnson's."[88]

Golden also used numerous anecdotes in the *Israelite* in order to illustrate his point of view. Under the theme of "gradualism" he wrote a series of anecdotes on the reluctance of many white southerners to embrace the idea of equality for blacks. In one instance, he commented on the men's room of the Hoke County, North Carolina courthouse. He noted that there were three stalls marked "white," "colored," and "Indian," yet there was only "one urinal."[89]

Similarly, on another occasion he commented on the emergency room of the Alachua County General Hospital in Gainesville, Florida. He explained that there were three thermometers in a row on a small shelf. The first one was labeled "white-oral," and the second "colored-oral," However, he noted the third thermometer was simply labeled "rectal." According to Golden, "This is what I call gradual integration."[90]

In another series of anecdotes Golden asserted that not only did whites treat blacks as second-class citizens, but some other minority groups also treated blacks poorly. He believed that this was the case because no one liked being the "low man on the totem pole."[91] For example, he asserted "The Puerto Ricans of New York are telling their children to keep speaking Spanish so they will not be mistaken for Negroes."[92] He also related the following story to illustrate his contention. There was a restaurant in Nevada which was owned by a Chinese couple. The cashier was "Anglo-Saxon," the waitresses "all Mexicans," the bus girls were "Navajo Indians," and the janitor was "an exchange student from India." Despite "all that color on board" when a black family attempted to eat at the restaurant they were run out by the "Chinese proprietor" who yelled, "No cullah here, no cullah."[93]

Golden's concern about the use of color as a barrier between human beings led to other anecdotes. For example, he used the story of a dog owner in Georgia to stress the absurdity of color barriers. In this story, the color of the owner of a dead dog was the factor used to determine the section of a pet cemetery in which the dog could be buried. Golden contended that a black dog owned by a white man could be buried in the "white dog" section. However, a white dog owned by a black man had to be buried in the "colored dog" section.[94]

Golden also used anecdotes to comment on the variety of responses of whites and businesses to sit-ins. He revealed that some white store managers closed the lunch counters of their stores to prevent sit-ins.[95] However, he also described a unique approach taken by one Charlotte store. According to Golden, as one viewed the lunch counter of this store it looked as though it was surrounded by "enamelled palings." Upon closer inspection the "palings" were really counter stools with the seats taken off. When whites wanted something to eat they merely had to request a seat top from a white waitress and "she would hand it to you, and you screwed it on and sat down."[96] The waitresses would "hover over" the customers while they ate. As soon as the customer finished eating the waitress would "lean across the counter top and quickly grab the detachable seat."[97] Thus "only the sharp iron bar" was left for the black demonstrators.[98] In another sit-in story, Golden discussed how the tables were turned on whites during a sit-in. In this case, a group of whites decided to stage a protest of their own against black sit-in demonstrators. The whites followed the blacks to a department store. However, the store manager thought they were with the blacks. Consequently, the police were called and the whites were ejected from the store. When they tried to explain their anti-black position to the store manager, he accused them of being "infiltrators."[99]

The protocol of segregation was intriguing to Golden. He believed that such protocol was "highly complicated" and caused people to do "unnatural things." Therefore, Golden often commented on it. In one such anecdote he discussed the way for whites to drive their black maids to and from work. According to Golden, southern tradition dictated that when picking up the maid she would sit in the front seat of the car. The back seat was always reserved for "family, friends, and important guests."[100] Golden asserted that southerners also believed that it was not socially correct for a white to sit next to a black. Therefore, he noted that whites usually took their children with them when picking up the maid. Thus, the children sat in the back and the maid in the front without impropriety. Such an arrangement indicated to all onlookers that the black was not a distinguished guest, but indeed a maid.[101] Golden also pointed out flaws in this system. For example, he questioned, if there were no children, would a white couple have children just for the sake of driving the maid? Golden also wondered, what if there were two maids? He noted that a white driver would look like a chauffeur if the two maids sat in the back seat. Golden continued, "My readers on Mars will never believe any of this."[102]

Non-Humorous Commentary

Although Golden was known for his use of satire, he also used non-humorous commentary when advocating civil rights through the *Israelite*. With such commentary, he presented his ideas and reactions on a variety of race related topics in a clear, concise manner. For example, on the issues of equality and civil rights he wrote:

> Equality means the opportunity to become full citizens. Negro roots are deep in American culture. He only asks that these roots be allowed to send up shoots of aspiration that will blossom in fulfillment.[103]

> Civil rights is theirs [blacks] by reason of birth on American soil. They are not storming the castle or the cathedral to get something that belongs to someone else. They are marching to get something which belongs to them.[104]

Golden also commented on segregation noting:

> Racial segregation violates every known principle of Anglo-Saxon law because of double jeopardy. The individual is twice segregated. First by the segregation itself and second by the attitude of society.[105]

In terms of white perceptions of blacks and the reality of black life, Golden noted:

> White ideas of the Negro have in large part been formed by antecedent white men talking about Negro sex maniacs or wearing black-face and singing "Mammy." Most Negroes are intent on paying off a mortgage, buying life insurance, and hoping to save enough to educate their children.[106]

Golden reacted to the poor treatment of blacks by the legal system in the South with the following comments:

On the surface, the Negro would appear to receive equal justice. Many southern judges are scrupulously fair. Others seem to view themselves less as impartial umpires and dispensers of justice than as defenders of white supremacy. Often the Negro accused of a major crime is forced to accept a court-appointed white attorney with little enthusiasm for his case. The ultimate responsibility is with the people to assure liberty and justice for all--in the South and across the nation wherever dual justice prevails.[107]

Golden wrote the following comments in response to the national outcry surrounding the deaths of white civil rights workers such as Andrew Goodman, Michael Schwerner, Viola Liuzzo, and James Reeb:[108]

[D]o you have any idea how many black bodies, black half-bodies, black headless bodies, are rotting in the swamps of Louisiana, Alabama, and Mississippi?[109]

[A]las, we ought to remember the hundreds upon hundreds of blacks who disappeared without an obituary or a mourner to sorrow for their deaths.[110]

[B]lacks were smart to encourage the participation of the white clergy, and the white men and women freedom riders. Martin Luther King once told me, "They look for white bodies." He was right.[111]

Golden responded to the progress of the right for civil rights and warned against complacency with the following comments:

It is easy to say that much has been done for the Negro and that now is the time for a breather. But while we catch our breath, Negroes in the deep South are being terrorized for sending their children to desegregated

> schools. Some are being victimized by white supremacists and juries. Many are being denied a chance to compete on equal terms for decent jobs.[112]

Golden primarily utilized the satiric humor of his Jewish heritage as a weapon in the fight for black civil rights. His satire took various forms, such as plans and anecdotes. In addition, he also used non-satiric advocacy. Despite the various forms of journalistic advocacy, Golden's message of equality for blacks prevailed. Indeed, as a result of his advocacy through the *Israelite* he was in demand as a speaker and as a television/radio personality.

Television and Radio Commentary

Golden made numerous appearances on national, regional, and local television and radio shows. He took such opportunities, via the broadcast media, to spread the same messages of hope, peace, tolerance, and understanding that he had already presented through the print media. He appeared on all of the major television networks of the time (NBC, CBS, ABC) and was even offered the opportunity to appear on the short-lived Dumont Broadcasting Corporation television network. Likewise, Golden was heard on all of the major radio networks of the era (NBC, CBS, ABC) as well as the Mutual Broadcasting System. Included among the TV shows on which Golden appeared were The Today Show and The Tonight Show on NBC (where appeared several times). Other shows included: The Merv Griffin Show, The Mike Douglas Show, The David Frost Show, Firing Line with William F. Buckley, Person to Person with

Edward R. Murrow, Open End with David Susskind, etc. Golden also made numerous national and local radio appearances.[113]

Opposition and the Closing of the Carolina Israelite

Opposition Without

Golden faced varied opposition to his civil rights advocacy through the *Israelite*. According to Golden, the typical response of southern white gentiles to the *Israelite* was in the form of comments such as "What is that fat little Jew doing coming down here telling us about our Negroes?"[114] However, the reaction of southern white gentiles often took the form of harassment. The harassment included obscene hate mail and abusive late night telephone calls.[115] Golden also received death threats by mail and telephone.[116]

Golden considered all hate mail a "sad manifestation of insanity."[117] He revealed that one hate mail writer regularly wrote, in red crayon, "Kill all the nigger-loving Jews."[118] Another hate mail writer described Golden as "a champion of niggers."[119] According to Golden, hate mail senders even used obscenities in writing the address on the envelope. He asserted that they believed their messages, thereby, were seen by a wider audience such as postal employees and the secretary who handled the mail. Golden believed that writers of such mail labored under the false assumption that he read the letters with "trembling hands and a racing pulse."[120] He also revealed that hate mail was used more successfully by white bigots to pressure his local advertisers. As a result, he lost local advertising revenue and at one time had to borrow money to keep the paper going.[121]

Golden considered abusive late night telephone calls more annoying than hate mail. One night he answered the telephone and the caller accused him of being a "nigger lover" and threatened to shoot him "right between the eyes."[122] Golden also described another series of telephone calls. This time the caller continually telephoned him over a six-month period and during each call asked him, "Why are you doing this to us [whites]? Why do you take up for the Negroes?" Golden finally replied, in jest, "Why shouldn't I take up for the Negroes? I am half Negro."[123] Despite Golden's humorous response to this caller, he considered such telephone callers, as well as hate mail writers, bigoted cowards who used phony names and reveled in the security of their anonymity.[124]

Golden also encountered opposition from the local Charlotte Jewish community. According to Golden, the Charlotte Jews considered him "dangerous and insane."[125] He argued that local Jews always feared that one Jew might say or do something that would involve the entire Jewish community.[126] Therefore, they feared that the white gentiles might believe that Golden and the *Israelite* spoke for the local Jewish community. Consequently, Golden revealed that many of Charlotte's Jewish business owners, who feared a loss of business or other reprisals, urged him to give up the paper.[127] However, Golden asserted that despite the fear, the Jews could not find a moral argument against his civil rights advocacy.[128]

Golden revealed that some members of the Jewish community questioned his civil rights advocacy through the *Israelite* because of their perception of anti-semitism in the black community. In response, Golden stressed that, as a people, blacks suffered from the same faults and vices--hatred, greed--as other groups. He, likewise, emphasized that blacks shared "the same virtues as humanity everywhere."[129]

Golden credited his eventual reprieve from the ire of his fellow North Carolina Jews to the friendship extended him by Dr. Frank Porter Graham, the president of the University of North Carolina at Chapel Hill. Graham, an influential white gentile, openly supported Golden's civil rights advocacy in the *Israelite*. According to Golden, when his friendship with Graham became public knowledge, the Jewish community in Charlotte "ceased and desisted"[130] in their criticism because he had the stamp of approval of an influential white gentile.[131]

Despite the opposition of many southern Jews and white gentiles, Golden's fame continued to grow. He received positive reinforcement of his advocacy,[132] especially on the national level. Many people considered Golden a responsible critic of racism and a civil rights spokesman.[133]

Ironically, in 1958, Golden became a victim of his own fame when opposition took the form of a strategically placed anonymous letter.[134] The letter, a copy of which was sent to the *New York Herald Tribune*, revealed that Golden was an ex-convict.[135] According to Golden, among other things, the unsigned letter said "Do you know that Harry Golden is a swindler, a cheat, and ex-con, and jail bird who has victimized widows and orphans?"[136]

Golden had kept his past imprisonment a secret, known only to a few people, prior to becoming famous. Therefore, the public revelation of his past through a *Herald Tribune* article[137] caused him great embarrassment. In addition, he did not want the publicity about prison to obscure or detract from the importance of the civil rights movement.[138]

Golden was afraid that white racists would say, "There is one of your leaders who is nothing but an ex-convict."[139]

Golden was surprised when the press, instead of scorning him, praised him for bouncing back and doing well after prison. Max Lerner of the *New York Post* captured the sentiment of the time when he wrote:

> Who dares sit in judgment on a man like this, whose energies have been spent in joyous attack on so many hypocrisies in American life. . . ? Every day, every moment of his life, a man is renewed because he is washing away the past in the stream of the present. Whatever Harry Golden once was, he is no rake now. He does not have to prove he is a new man.[140]

With such support, Golden was inspired to continue his advocacy of civil rights with a new zeal, because a burden he had carried for many years was finally lifted. The opposition from without failed to destroy Golden.

Opposition Within

In the late 1960s, with the advent of the Black Power movement,[141] some segments of the fight for civil rights turned away from the passive, nonviolent, resistance of the earlier days of the movement and toward black militancy.[142] Consequently, Golden began to oppose the direction of those segments of the civil rights movement. These strategic changes caused him to lose his zeal for continuing the fight for civil rights. The onslaught of black militancy caused Golden to lose his sense of humor concerning the movement. According to Golden, "The romance has gone from the civil rights movement. It went out the day the black militant came in."[143] He also noted, "There is nothing funny about it anymore nor do I attempt to find its humor."[144] As a Jew, Golden was personally offended by the black power movement. He believed that black power leaders such as H. Rap Brown and Stokely Carmichael advocated violence and hatred toward all whites, including Jews.[145]

Golden also became disenchanted because he believed that militancy was not only wrong but would lead to a backlash by whites. He indicated that in the early days of the movement, thousands of whites did not think it was right to speak out against civil rights because:

> How could they fight a group of Negroes kneeling on the sidewalk in front of Woolworth's praying to be allowed to eat at the snack bar? How could they fight a Negro protest which was using Christianity as a weapon for social justice?[146]

Golden believed that black militancy would lead to racial polarization and the elimination of a movement that was pushing ahead and gaining success. According to Golden, "With polarization comes the elimination of protests, no more sit-ins or parades, no forward movement, no movement of any kind."[147] He asserted that the civil rights struggle would become more difficult with no end in sight because both the segregationist and the black militant were menaces to equity.[148]

Golden's humor and spirit were also adversely affected by the 1968 assassinations of two friends, Martin Luther King, Jr. and Robert F. Kennedy.[149] Golden believed that the deaths of King and Kennedy were devastating to the civil rights movement because both King and Kennedy were central and important heroes with whom blacks and whites could relate. According to Golden, King chose religion as the vehicle to unify blacks and whites, while Kennedy chose politics, pressure groups, and lobbies.[150] He noted, "with King gone, equity for all will not come through a religious crusade; with Kennedy gone, it will not come through political innovation."[151]

Harry Golden closed the *Carolina Israelite* in February of 1968. He rationalized that he was losing money on the paper, he was getting too old to run the paper, and his audience was also growing old and dying off.[152] But, as discussed, the opposition from within had taken its toll on Golden.

Golden curtailed his activity during the late 1960s and 1970s after suffering a stroke. He died of congestive heart failure in October of 1981.[153] However, through the use of the *Carolina Israelite* during the 1950s and 1960s he facilitated equity for all by positively influencing the way many people thought about civil rights and racial equality.

Chapter Two Notes

[1]Harry Golden, "25th Anniversary" *Carolina Israelite* Nov.-Dec. 1966: 8; Harry Golden, *The Right Time: An Autobiography, by Harry Golden* (New York: Putnam, 1969) 255. Golden also contended that the first regular issue of the *Israelite* was produced in February of 1942, See Golden "25th Anniversary" 8. However, according to others (including) Robin Brabham, the head of the Harry Golden collection at the U of North Carolina at Charlotte, the Library of Congress, and the Interlibrary Loan system, the first issue of the *Israelite*--vol. 1, no. 1--is dated February 1944. Brabham and Golden's son, William Goldhurst, suggest that if pre-1944 issues of the *Israelite* did exist they were probably destroyed in a 1958 fire

which gutted Golden's home and office. Source: Robin Brabham, letter to Delores Jenkins, 21 Nov. 1989, Author's files; William Goldhurst, personal interview, 30 March 1990; Harry Golden, "Serials Search" *Library of Congress DCLC/RLIN regular and bibliographic record* April 1990: (DCLC 79645468-S); Harry Golden, "Serials Search" *Interlibrary loan multiple screen* April 1990. Also see Harry Golden, *For 2 Cents Plain* (Cleveland: World, 1958) 17.

[2]Harry Golden, *The Best of Harry Golden* (Cleveland: World, 1967) 16; Golden, *The Right Time* 255.

[3]William Goldhurst, personal interview, 30 March 1990.

[4]See for example: Harry Golden, "Anti-semitism," "Fighting Jews," and "History of Jews in America" in *Carolina Israelite* Feb. 1944: 4, 7, 8.

[5]See for example, the banner of *Carolina Israelite* Jan. 1947: 1.

[6]See Chapter 1 for a discussion of Golden's concern about the plight of blacks in Charlotte.

[7]Harry Golden, interview, *Sunday Morning*. CBS TV 25 October 1981; Golden, *The Right Time* 251.

[8]Harry Golden, *Unity in America* (Cleveland: World, 1958) 15.

[9]Personal Journalists are self employed members of the press who practice personal journalism--social commentary, advocacy of causes--instead of reporting typical news events. They usually operate small publications where they perform a variety of duties such as writing and editing. Golden once described personal journalists as "journalistic jack-of-all-trades." See Harry Golden,"The Topic of the Times," *Carolina Israelite* Dec. 1957: 11. By his own admission, Golden was a personal journalist. See Golden, The Right Time 364.

[10]Golden, *Unity in America* 16.

[11]Golden, *The Right Time* 251.

[12]Golden, *The Right Time* 252.

[13]Golden, *The Right Time* 252.

[14]Golden, *The Right Time* 251-252. According to Golden, his readership included Christian and Jewish religious leaders; government and political leaders; business and industry leaders; newspaper publishers, editors, and writers; lawyers and doctors; and many of the famous people of the time. See Harry Golden, "Readership," *Carolina Israelite* March/April 1959: 9; and Golden, *Unity in America* 13. In addition, readership ranged from 400 in 1941 to 53,000 in 1959 and reached 49 states and 33 foreign countries. See Golden, "25th Anniversary" 8; Harry Golden, "Net Circulation," *Carolina Israelite* Oct. 1959: 12; Harry Golden, "Net Circulation," *Carolina Israelite* May 1959: 9; and Harry Golden, "The Carolina Israelite's Printing," *Carolina Israelite* Feb. 1957: 1.

[15]Haldeman-Julius was a prolific writer and publisher. In addition to the *American Freeman* his numerous other periodicals included: *Life and Letters, The Critic and Guide*, the *Haldeman-Julius Weekly*, the *Haldeman-Julius Monthly*, the *Haldeman-Julius Quarterly, Questions and Answers, Notes and Comments, Views and Reviews, Little Blue Books*, and *Big Blue Books*. See Emanuel Haldeman-Julius, *The First Hundred Million* (New York: Simon and Schuster, 1928) 1-12, 179-221; Albert Mordell. "E. Haldeman-Julius--His Career and Personality," *American Freeman* Nov. 1951: 1; Albert Mordell, *The World of Haldeman-Julius* (New York: Twayne, 1960) 19, 21, 30, 31; David White, ed. *Little Blue Books* (New York: Arno, 1974) 1-2; and Golden, *The Right Time* 252; "Little Blue Books," *Time* 15 Aug. 1960: 38, 39.

[16]Harry Golden, foreword, *The World of Haldeman-Julius* by Albert Mordell (New York: Twayne, 1960) 5-7; Mordell, *The World of Haldeman-Julius* 9, 23, 25; Harry Golden, "Haldeman-Julius--The Success that Failed," *Midstream: A Quarterly Jewish Review* 3.2 (1957): 28; Harry Golden, letter to M. Grusd, 30 Sept. 1951, Box 24 File 150, Harry Golden Collection Part II, U of North Carolina, Charlotte.

[17]John Gunn, "My Friend Emanuel," *The American Freeman* Nov. 1951: 1.

[18]Mordell, *The World of Haldeman-Julius* 22; Mordell, "E. Haldeman-Julius--His Career and Personality" 1.

[19]Golden, *The Right Time* 255.

[20]E. Haldeman-Julius, "One of My Readers," *The American Freeman* July 1951: 1; Mordell, *The World of Haldeman-Julius* 22, 24; Golden, *The Right Time* 253; Harry Golden, "Emanuel Haldeman-Julius," *Carolina Israelite* Jan./Feb. 1968: 8.

[21]Harry Golden, letter to William Ryan, 28 July 1969, Box 8 File 27, Harry Golden Collection Part II, U of North Carolina at Charlotte; William Ryan, letter to Harry Golden, 25 July 1969, Box 8 File 27, Harry Golden Collection Part II, U of North Carolina at Charlotte.

[22]Golden, *The Right Time* 252, 255; Golden, "Emanuel Haldeman-Julius" 8.

[23]E. Haldeman-Julius, letters to Harry Golden, 28 Jan. 1951, 8 Mar. 1951, and 12 May 1951, Box 8 File 26, Harry Golden Collection Part II, U of North Carolina at Charlotte; Mordell, *The World of Haldeman-Julius* 24.

[24]Golden, "Haldeman-Julius--The Success that Failed," 26, 30; Golden, *The Right Time* 252, 255.

[25]Emanuel Haldeman-Julius, "Writers," *The American Freeman* May 1951: 2.

[26]Mordell, *The World of Haldeman-Julius* 9.

[27]Emanuel Haldeman-Julius, *America's Fakirs and Guides*, Little Blue Book Series 1288 (Girard: Haldeman-Julius, 1928) 9.

[28]Mordell, *The World of Haldeman-Julius* 156.

[29]Mordell, *The World of Haldeman-Julius* 159.

[30]William Goldhurst, "My Father, Harry Golden," *Midstream* June/July 1969: 68, 73; William Goldhurst, personal interview, 30 March 1990.

[31]Harry Golden, *The Golden Book of Jewish Humor* (New York: Putnam, 1972) 11.

[32]William Goldhurst, personal interview, 30 March 1990.

[33]Golden, *The Golden Book of Jewish Humor* 12.

[34]Harry Golden, "Jewish Wit," *Carolina Israelite* Dec. 1965: 5.

[35]Golden, "Jewish Wit," 5.

[36]Golden, *The Golden Book of Jewish Humor* 12.

[37]Golden, *The Golden Book of Jewish Humor* 16.

[38]William Goldhurst, personal interview, 30 March 1990; Golden, *The Golden Book of Jewish Humor* 11.

[39]*Oliver Brown v. Board of Education of Topeka, Kansas,* 74 S. St. 686 and 347 U.S. 483, 1954. Also see Appendix A for a discussion of *Brown v. Board.*

[40]Harry Golden, "How to Survive the Segregation Problem," *Carolina Israelite* June 1956: 1.

[41]Golden, "How to Solve" 1.

[42]Golden, "How to Solve" 1; Golden, *Only in America* 121; Golden, *The Best of Harry Golden* 219-221.

[43]Harry Golden, "The Peculiar Institution," *Carolina Israelite* Sept./Oct. 1960: 6; Harry Golden, *So What Else is New?* (New York: Putnam, 1964) 97.

[44]Harry Golden, "The Golden Out-of-Order Plan," *Carolina Israelite* Feb. 1957: 1; Harry Golden, "Gradual Desegregation," *Carolina Israelite* Nov. 1958: 9; Golden, *Only in America* 123.

[45]Harry Golden, "How to solve the segregation problem: The White Baby Plan," *Carolina Israelite* March/April 1957: 1; Golden, *Only in America* 122-123.

[46]See Appendix A for a discussion of the "Little Rock Nine."

[47]Harry Golden, "The Golden Carry-the-Books Plan," *Carolina Israelite* Jan./Feb. 1958: 7; Golden, *Unity in America* 124.

[48]Harry Golden, "Solve the Race Problem and Revive Textiles," *Carolina Israelite* Aug. 1958: 3; Harry Golden, "My Turban Plan and Sir Fitzroy," *Carolina Israelite* Feb. 1962: 9; Harry Golden, "The Turban is a Very Big Thing," *Carolina*

Israelite Aug. 1956: 8; Harry Golden, *You're Entitle'* (Cleveland: World, 1962) 200-202; Golden, *The Best of Harry Golden* 228; Golden, *Unity in America* 155.

[49]See Appendix A and/or Appendix B for information on the White Citizens Councils.

[50]See note #38.

[51]Golden, *Only in America* 139.

[52]Harry Golden, "A Plan to Revive the Motion Picture Business in the South," *Carolina Israelite* Feb. 1959: 5; Golden, *You're Entitle'* 201.

[53]Harry Golden, "The Golden Pogo Stick Plan," *Carolina Israelite* April 1959: 2; Golden, *For 2 Cents Plain* 275.

[54]Harry Golden, "A Plan to end Racial Segregation," *Carolina Israelite* Aug. 1959: 11.

[55]Golden, *The Best of Harry Golden* 237.

[56]Golden, *For 2 Cents Plain* 278.

[57]Harry Golden, "We Are Color-Happy," *Carolina Israelite* Sept./Oct. 1960: 12.

[58]Golden, "We Are Color-Happy" 12.

[59]Golden, "We Are Color-Happy" 12.

[60]Golden, "We Are Color-Happy" 12.

[61]Golden, "We Are Color-Happy" 12.

[62]Golden, "We Are Color-Happy" 12.

[63]Golden, "We Are Color-Happy" 12.

[64]Harry Golden, "The New Drugs--An Easy End to Segregation," *Carolina Israelite* Mar./April 1961: 17. Dihydroxyactone ($C_3H_6O_3$) is an actual drug.

[65]Golden, "The New Drugs" 17.

[66]Harry Golden, "A New Golden Plan to End Racial Segregation," *Carolina Israelite* July/Aug. 1961: 1; Golden, *You're Entitle'* 210-211.

[67]Golden, "A New Golden Plan" 1; Golden, <u>You're Entitle'</u> 210-211.

[68]Harry Golden, "Another Modest Proposal," <u>Carolina Israelite</u> July/Aug. 1962: 4.

[69]Golden, "Another Modest Proposal" 4.

[70]Golden, "Another Modest Proposal" 4.

[71]Golden, "Another Modest Proposal" 4.

[72]Golden, "Another Modest Proposal" 4.

[73]Golden, *You're Entitle'* 201.

[74]Golden, *You're Entitle'* 201.

[75]Harry Golden, "Let's Put it to the Test," *Carolina Israelite* Sept./Oct. 1963: 16.

[76]Harry Golden, "The Golden Vertical Insurance Plan," *Carolina Israelite* Sept./Oct. 1964: 15; Harry Golden, *Ess, Ess Mein Kindt* (New York: Putnam, 1966) 164-165; Golden, *The Best of Harry Golden* 260-261.

[77]Harry Golden, "Goodbye," *Carolina Israelite* Jan.Feb. 1968: 5; Harry Golden, "Smorgasbord is Running the Golden Vertical Plan," *Carolina Israelite* May/June 1961: 9; Harry Golden, "The Golden Vertical Plan in Reverse," *Carolina Israelite* Nov./Dec. 1960: 18.

[78]Harry Golden, "The Golden Vertical Negro Plan in Operation," *Carolina Israelite* Sept./Oct. 1957: 1.

[79]Harry Golden, "The Vertical Plan in Operation," *Carolina Israelite* Sept./Oct. 1960: 9.

[80]Harry Golden, "The Vertical Plan," *Carolina Israelite* July/Aug. 1962: 8.

[81]Harry Golden, "Indoors--Vertical Negro, Outdoors--Sittin' Down," *Carolina Israelite* May/June 1963: 1.

[82]Golden, *You're Entitle'* 202.

[83]Golden, "My Turban Plan and Sir Fitzroy" 9.

[84]Golden, *You're Entitle'* 202; Golden, "My Turban Plan and Sir Fitzroy" 9.

[85]Golden, "The Golden Out-of-Order Plan" 1; Harry Golden, "Golden Out-of-Order Plan in Operation," *Carolina Israelite* June 1958: 1; Golden, *Only in America* 123.

[86]See Appendix A for a discussion of Eugene "Bull" Connor.

[87]Harry Golden, "The Bull Connor Award," *Carolina Israelite* May/June 1963: 12.

[88]Harry Golden, "The Pickets Are Getting 30 Days in Jail," *Carolina Israelite* Sept./Oct. 1962: 12.

[89]Harry Golden, "Gradual Integration," *Carolina Israelite* May/June 1962: 10.

[90]Harry Golden, "Alachua General Hospital," *Carolina Israelite* Jan./Feb. 1962: 1.

[91]Harry Golden, "The Need for a Low Man on the Totem Pole," *Carolina Israelite* Aug. 1958: 8.

[92]Golden, "The Need" 8.

[93]Harry Golden, "No One Here but Us Chickens," *Carolina Israelite* Nov./Dec. 1961: 18.

[94]Harry Golden, *So Long as You're Healthy* (New York: Putnam, 1970) 152; Harry Golden, "We Are All Colorless," *Carolina Israelite* Dec. 1958: 1; Harry Golden, "How About the Black Ink," *Carolina Israelite* May/June 1960: 24.

[95]Harry Golden, "The Sit-ins provided Some Excellent American Humor," *Carolina Israelite* Sept./Oct. 1960: 2.

[96]Harry Golden, "The Sit-in Demonstrations," *Carolina Israelite* March/April 1960: 5.

[97]Golden, "The Sit-ins Produced" 2; Golden, "The Sit-in Demonstrations" 5.

[98]Golden, "The Sit-ins Produced" 2.

[99]Golden, "The Sit-ins Produced" 2.

[100]Harry Golden, "The Negro Maid and Protocol," *Carolina Israelite* Jan./Feb. 1960: 14.

[101]Golden, "The Negro Maid" 14.

[102]Golden, "The Negro Maid" 14.

[103]Harry Golden, "The Revolution," *Carolina Israelite* Sept./Oct. 1963: 4.

[104]Harry Golden, "The Negro Protests," *Carolina Israelite* July/Aug. 1963: 1.

[105]Harry Golden, "Racial Segregation," *Carolina Israelite* Aug. 1955: 5.

[106]Harry Golden, "The New Man," *Carolina Israelite* Nov./Dec. 1963: 13.

[107]Harry Golden, "Southern Justice and the Negro," *Carolina Israelite* Nov./Dec. 1965: 15.

[108]See Appendix A for information on murdered civil rights workers.

[109]Harry Golden, "Why didn't she stay home?" *Carolina Israelite* May/June 1965: 26.

[110]Harry Golden, "What's Behind it All?" *Carolina Israelite* Aug. 1964: 4.

[111]Golden, "Why Didn't She" 26.

[112]Harry Golden, "The Future of Civil Rights," *Carolina Israelite* April/May 1967: 16.

[113]Radio Files, 1961-1971, Series 6 Box 1 Sub-series 1, Harry Golden Collection, Part II, U of North Carolina at Charlotte; Morton Silverstein/Dumont Broadcasting Corp., letter to Harry Golden, 17 March 1958, Series 2 Box 19, Harry Golden Collection, Part II, U of North Carolina at Charlotte; NBC Today Show Files, 1963-1970, Series 6 Sub-series 1, Harry Golden Collection, Part II, U of North Carolina at Charlotte; NBC Tonight Show Files, 1962-1966, Series 6 Sub-series 1, Harry Golden Collection, Part II, U of North Carolina at Charlotte; Merv Griffin Show Files, 1967-1970, Series 6 Box 1 Sub-series 1, Harry Golden Collection, Part II, U of North Carolina at Charlotte; Mike Douglas Show Files, 1964-1970, Series 6 Box 1 Sub-series 1, Harry Golden Collection, Part II, U of North Carolina at Charlotte; David Rubin, letter to Harry Golden, 15 Sept. 1969, Series 7 Box 1, Harry Golden Collection, Part II, U of North Carolina at Charlotte; William F. Buckley/Firing Line Files, 1966, Series 6 Box 1 Sub-series 1, Harry Golden Collection, Part II, U of North Carolina at Charlotte; Edward R. Murrow/Person to Person Files, 1960, Series 6 Box 1 Sub-series 1, Harry Golden Collection, Part II, U of North Carolina at Charlotte; David Susskind, letter to Harry Golden, 8 June 1959, Box 60, Harry Golden Collection, Part I, U of North Carolina at Charlotte.

[114]Golden, *The Right Time* 256.

[115]Harry Golden, "My Critics," *Carolina Israelite* July/Aug. 1965: 30; Golden, *The Right Time* 256; Harry Golden, *Ess, Ess Mein Kindt* 217; Harry Golden, "The Pressure on the Carolina Israelite" *Carolina Israelite* Oct. 1957: 4; Golden, *So What Else is New* 16.

[116]Harry Golden, letters to Agent in Charge FBI, 17 Mar. 1959 and 30 Aug. 1962, Box 7 File 11, Harry Golden Collection Part II, U of North Carolina at Charlotte.

[117]Harry Golden, "Hate Mail," *Carolina Israelite* July/Aug. 1962: 8.

[118]Golden, "Hate Mail" 8; Golden, *Ess, Ess, Mein Kindt* 217.

[119]Anonymous post card to Harry Golden, 4 Aug. 1961, Box 2 File 12, Harry Golden Collection Part II, U of North Carolina at Charlotte.

[120]Golden, "Hate Mail" 8.

[121]Golden, *The Right Time* 309-311. Golden later made up the loss of local advertising through his book royalties, lecture fees, outside advertising, and national circulation.

[122]Harry Golden, letter to Agent in Charge FBI, 30 Aug. 1962, Box 7 File 11, Harry Golden Collection Part II, U of North Carolina at Charlotte.

[123]Golden *Ess, Ess, Mein Kindt* 218.

[124]Golden, "Hate Mail" 8.

[125]Golden, *The Right Time* 265.

[126]Golden, *Only in America* 16; See Chapter 1 for a discussion of Golden's views on southern Jewry and black civil rights.

[127]Golden, *The Right Time* 264; Golden was also attacked by the Jewish publication *Commentary*. He was accused of superficial advocacy. See Theodore Solotaroff, "Harry Golden and the American Audience," *Commentary* Jan. 1961: 1-13; Harold Ribalow, "Commentary vs. Harry Golden," *Congress Bi-Weekly* 13 Feb. 1961: 9-11.

[128]Golden, *The Right Time* 265.

[129]Golden, *So What Else is New?* 79.

[130]Golden, *The Right Time* 266.

[131]Golden, *The Right Time* 266-267.

[132]See Chapters 3 and 4 for a discussion of the influence and impact of Golden's civil rights advocacy.

[133]William Goldhurst, personal interview, 30 March 1990.

[134]Anonymous letter to World Publishing Company, 13 Sept. 1958, Box 32 File 285, Harry Golden Collection Part I, University of North Carolina, Charlotte.

[135]Golden, *For 2 Cents Plain* 19; *The Right Time* 348.

[136]Golden, *The Right Time* 348.

[137]Judith Crist, "Golden, Best Seller Author, Reveals His Prison Past," *New York Herald Tribune* 18 Sept. 1958: 1, 11.

[138]Golden, *For 2 Cents Plain* 19.

[139]Golden, *The Right Time* 350.

[140]Max Lerner, "The Secret Place," *New York Post* 21 Sept. 1958: M8; Also see "The Golden Story," *Time* 29 Sept. 1958: 72.

[141]See Appendix A for a discussion of the civil rights movement.

[142]David Garrow, *Bearing the Cross: Martin Luther King, Jr. and the Southern Christian Leadership Conference* (New York: Vintage, 1988) 475.

[143]Golden, "Goodbye" 2.

[144]Golden, "Goodbye" 2.

[145]Harry Golden, "Black Power," *Carolina Israelite* July/Aug. 1966: 2; Harry Golden, "What is Black Power?" *Carolina Israelite* Nov./Dec. 1966: 10-11; Golden, *The Right Time* 395; Gus Solomon, *The Jewish Role in the American Civil Rights Movement* (London: The World Jewish Congress, 1967) 24.

[146]Golden, *So Long as You're Healthy* 143.

[147]Golden, "What is Black Power" 11.

[148]Golden, "Black Power" 2.

[149]See Chapter 3 for a discussion of the relationship between Golden, the Kennedys, and Martin Luther King, Jr.

[150]Golden, *So Long as You're Healthy* 164.

[151]Golden, *The Right Time* 15.

[152]Golden, "Goodbye" 1; Douglas Robinson, "Harry Golden: On Things Remembered," *New York Times* 26 Feb. 1968: 36.

[153]Anita Brown, telephone interview, 6 June 1990.

CHAPTER THREE

THE PRIZE: GOLDEN'S APPEAL AND SIGNIFICANCE

Harry Golden had a positive influence on the way that many Americans viewed civil rights for blacks. His appeal crossed racial, religious, economic, and geographic boundaries. His advocacy was also appealing to many of the people who had a direct bearing on the course and outcome of the civil rights movement--America's civil rights and governmental leaders.

Golden and the Civil Rights Community

Civil Rights Organizations

Golden interacted with the civil rights community on a regular basis. In addition, the *Israelite* was read by important members of the black civil rights community, many of whom became Golden's friends. His advocacy was appreciated by, and had impact on, the major civil rights leaders and organizations of the 1950's and 1960's.

Golden's reputation for civil rights advocacy led to various requests for his involvement with civil rights organizations. Both the Southern Christian Leadership Conference (SCLC) and the Congress of Racial Equality (CORE)[1] utilized Golden as a speaker at their respective national conventions.[2] Golden also served as a consultant to the SCLC. The SCLC sought to incorporate his influence into their various attempts to create "moral pressure"[3] on the federal government to provide more support--legislation, executive orders--for the civil rights struggle. Out of gratitude for his involvement, the SCLC once wrote to Golden, "We are grateful for the part you are playing in the freedom movement."[4]

Golden's involvement also extended to other civil rights organizations. He was an advisor to the Student Nonviolent Coordinating Committee (SNCC). He was also a life member of the National Association for the Advancement of Colored People (NAACP).[5]

As a SNCC member, Golden counseled college students on the use of nonviolent protest. He also allowed his home and the *Israelite* offices to be used as a rest stop for students and other civil rights workers on their way to and from protests in the South. As a NAACP member, he was regularly asked to serve on various panels and committees in order to elaborate on his views concerning racial understanding and equality.[6]

Civil Rights Leaders

Golden's advocacy through the *Israelite* also appealed to major civil rights leaders. A. Phillip Randolph was a reader of the *Israelite*. He also served with Golden and others on a White House Conference on civil rights during the Kennedy administration. As one aware of Golden's advocacy, Randolph frequently enlisted Golden's assistance in various civil rights causes.[7]

On one such occasion, Randolph sought Golden's assistance in publicizing the work of a newly formed organization, the Alabama Legal Defense Committee. The organization had been formed to provide legal assistance for blacks and other civil rights workers jailed in Mobile and Montgomery, Alabama. Golden agreed to serve on an advisory board of the committee. He also promised to write an article about the committee's work.[8]

Former NAACP Executive Director Roy Wilkins was also a reader of the *Israelite*. He appreciated Golden's work on behalf of blacks.[9] According to Wilkins:

> Harry Golden has succeeded in attacking the irrationality of racial discrimination with withering scorn which has had lasting effect. Few men have been able to effectively expose human foibles, while showing that they truly care for mankind. . . . He is a consummate humorist, a perceptive social critic, who during his full and uncommonly rich lifetime has become a new kind of protagonist for justice in our complicated society.[10]

Dr. Martin Luther King, Jr.--the acknowledged leader of the civil rights movement[11]--was a reader of the *Israelite* and held a "special affection"[12] for Golden and his advocacy. King considered Golden a committed contributor to the civil rights movement. Highly indicative of Golden's significance to the civil rights movement are comments made by King while incarcerated during the SCLC's Birmingham campaign.[13]

In King's "Letter from Birmingham City Jail" he responded to a critical joint statement made by a group of prominent white Alabama clergymen--Catholic, Protestant, Jewish. The clergymen questioned the use and timing of the SCLC demonstrations. They also accused the demonstrators of being outsiders and urged local blacks not to participate in the protest.[14]

In his response, King expressed his dismay at the stand taken by the clergymen. He had previously considered them "white moderates" and "men of genuine good will."[15] King wrote:

> I have been gravely disappointed with the white moderate. . . who constantly says "I agree with you and in the goal you seek, but I can't agree with your methods". . . who constantly advises the Negro to wait until a "more convenient season."[16]

> I have never yet engaged in a direct action movement that was "well timed," according to the timetable of those who have not suffered unduly from the disease of segregation. For years now I have heard the word "Wait!". . . . This "wait" has almost always meant "never."[17]

> We have waited for more than three hundred and forty years for our constitutional and God-given rights.[18]

King went on to qualify his views on whites and the civil rights movement. In the process he identified Golden as one of four whites whom he believed were significant contributors to the fight for civil rights. According to King:

> I am thankful that some of our white brothers have grasped the meaning of this social revolution and committed themselves to it.[19]

> They are still too small in quantity, but they are big in quality. Some like Ralph McGill, Lillian Smith, Harry Golden, and James Dabbs have written about our struggle in eloquent, prophetic, and understanding terms. [20]

> [T]hey have recognized the urgency of the moment and sensed the need for powerful "action" antidotes to combat the disease of segregation.[21]

King's belief in Golden's commitment to the fight for civil rights is also exemplified by the following. Upon King's selection for the Nobel Peace Prize in 1964, he decided to donate $25,000 of the cash prize to the civil rights movement. King sought to use the funds to help increase black voter registration, provide educational opportunity for leadership training in nonviolence, and promote public awareness of racial violence and brutality.[22] In order to accomplish these goals, King formed a new organization--the American Foundation on Nonviolence--to supervise the implementation of his ideas. King asked Golden to serve on the Board of Directors of the Foundation. Golden accepted King's invitation and served in the company of other distinguished members such as Ralph David Abernathy, Benjamin Hooks, Joseph Lowery, A. Phillip Randolph, and Andrew Young.[23]

King and Golden continued to correspond until King's assassination.[24] Golden was saddened by the death. He noted, "It is a sad day for the world and a sadder day for Americans."[25] He also commented, "Martin Luther King's life was too short, but it made ours fuller."[26]

Many other civil rights leaders were also inspired by Golden and his work. According to Julian Bond, formerly of SNCC, "...Golden attacked racism with humor!"[27] John Lewis, also formerly of SNCC, noted "...Golden must be looked upon as one of those individuals who in his own way, with his sense of humor, played a role in the movement."[28]

Andrew Young, formerly of SCLC, commented "I liked Harry Golden because Golden dealt with a complex issue by poking fun at it. He did more than reporting!"[29] C. T. Vivian, also formerly of SCLC, said that "Golden dealt with the stupidity of racism and segregation with humor and lightness. He had the ability to make people discuss and laugh at themselves at the same time. Humor of that sort, makes both parties laugh, and in the laughter, they can begin to relate."[30]

James Farmer, former head of CORE, considered Golden a "humanist," "humorist," and an "institution." To Farmer, Golden not only spoke for the Jewish community, "He spoke for all of us." Farmer thought that humor, or making people laugh was one of the ways to change custom and morays. According to Farmer, "nobody could do it better than Golden."[31]

Although the *Israelite* was not specifically targeted at blacks,[32] members and leaders of the major civil rights organizations[33] welcomed Golden as an ally. The black civil rights community not only appreciated his civil rights advocacy, they sought his advice and participation in matters such as attempts to place "moral pressure" on the federal government for assistance.

Golden and the Federal Government

Harry Golden as an individual cannot be credited with the direct actions of the federal government on behalf of securing and protecting civil rights for blacks. However,

Golden was a facilitator who, through the press, actively contributed to the collective "push" of the movement for correction of racial inequality. Many of the governmental leaders--Judicial, Executive, Legislative,--who were in positions to influence governmental response and action concerning civil rights were likewise positively influenced by Golden's journalistic civil rights advocacy. Such leaders found Golden's advocacy appealing and enlightening.

The Judicial Branch

The Court and Civil Rights. The United States Supreme Court's decision in *Brown v. Board of Education*[34] not only found separate-but-equal schools unconstitutional, it undermined institutionalized segregation. The practice of segregation suffered further damage and the civil rights movement gained significant momentum based on another Supreme Court decision. In 1956, during the midst of the Montgomery, Alabama bus boycott,[35] the Supreme Court ruled that segregation on public bus systems was illegal.[36] The Court's ruling gave the budding civil rights movement one of its earliest victories. Likewise, the victory provided impetus for movement leaders and organizations to advance toward the manifold battles ahead.[37]

Golden and the Court. Several Supreme Court Justices read the *Israelite*. For example, Chief Justice Earl Warren, Justice Felix Frankfurter, and Justice Arthur Goldberg were among Golden's readers.[38] In addition, Justices William O. Douglas and Hugo Black both read the *Israelite* and maintained close friendships with Golden. Black and Golden visited each other[39] and wrote frequently. On one such occasion, Black commented on Golden's writing style. He noted, "I have always marveled at your pithy method of saying a lot with a few words."[40] On another occasion, Black expressed concern about Golden's well-being.[41] He wrote, "I had not heard from you in so long that I was wondering how things were going with you."[42]

Black and Golden also corresponded about busing and neighborhood schools. Black informed Golden that the presence of neighborhood school cases before the Court prevented his specific discussion of the subject.[43] However, Black did provide Golden with general thoughts on the pros and cons of neighborhood schools:

> I attended neighborhood schools. . . . Neighborhood schools involve some things that are good and some that are not, just as most everything else in this world does. My father walked five miles to get to his nearest neighborhood school but even back then I would say that he was subjected to fewer hazards than are many children in our teeming cities today [in the late 1960s].[44]

Douglas considered Golden an "accomplished journalist, a serious social historian,"[45] and a "friend who espoused desegregation of the races."[46] Douglas believed that Golden's writing was "spiced with witty observations that cut through prejudices, hypocrisy, and bigotry."[47] He also believed that the *Israelite* made a "great contribution over the years."[48] According to Douglas, Golden searched for the common bond among people and aimed his writing only at people who used "power, arrogance, position, or influence to downgrade others or to relegate them to second-class citizenship."[49] Douglas was inspired by Golden. Likewise, Golden enjoyed urging judicial leaders such as Douglas and Black to fight against racism.[50]

The Executive Branch

Selected U.S. Presidents and Civil Rights. Several United States Presidents supported the civil rights struggle in different ways. In September of 1957, President Dwight D. Eisenhower authorized the use of federal military troops to maintain the peace and protect black high school students during the implementation of school desegregation plans in Little Rock, Arkansas. President John F. Kennedy also approved the use of federal troops to assist in the peaceful integration of the University of Mississippi in 1962 and the University of Alabama in 1963. Presidents Kennedy and Lyndon B. Johnson also supported the movement by using federal troops to quell violence against civil right demonstrators. In May of 1963, Kennedy dispatched soldiers to Birmingham, Alabama in response to bombings and violence surrounding the SCLC's Birmingham campaign. Similarly, in March of 1965, Johnson used federal troops to protect demonstrators in the Selma to Montgomery march.[51]

Kennedy and Johnson also supported the movement in other ways. Kennedy not only had his Attorney General, Robert F. Kennedy, and the Justice Department vigorously litigate civil rights cases,[52] he also proposed the enactment of civil rights legislation.[53] After Kennedy's assassination in 1963, Johnson continued in his footsteps by signing the Civil Rights Act of 1964[54] and proposing and signing the Voting Rights Act of 1965.[55] On the occasion of his proposal of the Voting Rights Act, Johnson voiced his concern for civil rights and stressed the need for such legislation before a joint session of Congress. He concluded his comments with the slogan of the movement, "We Shall Overcome."[56]

Golden and U.S. Presidents. Golden's journalistic civil rights advocacy led to his recognition by several United States Presidents. His advocacy was appealing to them and members of their administrations. In addition, he was personally held in high esteem by these Presidents. Golden corresponded with Harry Truman and Dwight Eisenhower during the early days of the *Israelite*. He also established a regular civil rights dialogue with President Kennedy. [57]

President Kennedy was a reader of the *Israelite* and a personal friend of Golden.[58] Golden corresponded, consulted, and visited with Kennedy both prior to and during Kennedy's Presidency.[59] Kennedy was well aware of and appreciated Golden's civil rights advocacy. Similarly, Golden considered Kennedy "exceptionally well informed on the race issue."[60] Golden also considered Kennedy "An emancipator of civil rights President" who was "committed to the social revolution of the American Negro."[61]

In addition to Golden's visits and correspondence with Kennedy, on at least two occasions Kennedy enlisted Golden's assistance in matters concerning civil rights. As a Senator from Massachusetts, Kennedy invited Golden to serve on an Advisory Committee of the Democratic Advisory Council in order to implement the civil rights proposals of the Democratic platform.[62]

As President of the United States, Kennedy invited Golden to participate in a White House civil rights conference. According to Kennedy, the conference was designed to "help the American Negro fulfill the rights which, after the long time of injustice, he is finally about to secure."[63] Golden participated in the event along with civil rights leaders such as Martin Luther King, Jr., A. Phillip Randolph, Roy Wilkins, Whitney Young, and Vernon Jordan.[64]

Kennedy's Attorney General and brother, Robert F. Kennedy, was also a reader of the *Israelite* and a close personal friend of Golden.[65] Robert Kennedy and Golden communicated regularly about the civil rights movement and visited each other often.[66] Kennedy's respect for Golden's civil rights advocacy led him to reveal to Golden "I have always been a great admirer of yours and what you have stood for."[67] Similarly, Golden was "fascinated"[68] by the civil rights work of Kennedy. According to Golden, when Kennedy encountered the wrongs of the South, he became outraged and took steps to make things better.[69]

Lyndon B. Johnson was a reader of the *Israelite* while a Senator from Texas, as John Kennedy's Vice President, and as President of the United States. Johnson's familiarity with Golden's advocacy eventually led to correspondence between them. On occasion Johnson sought and utilized Golden's consultation.[70] During Johnson's "War on Poverty," he asked Golden for ideas on the topic. In his comments to Johnson, Golden addressed poverty as "a problem for millions of Americans of all races, creeds, and political loyalties and inclinations."[71] However, Golden argued that the problem of poverty was of special consequence to blacks. He commented:

> [F]or nearly a century we [whites] proved we had the power to annul the Negro's simple human dignity. We have it in our power to withdraw the remnant of authority, particularly in housing, which still disallows the Negro's full participation in American civilization.[72]

Johnson contended that he shared Golden's views and would use them in the "War on Poverty."[73]

Johnson's Vice President, Hubert H. Humphrey, was also a long-time reader of the *Israelite* and friend of Golden. Humphrey considered Golden "a continuing source of renewed strength."[74] In addition, Humphrey was a self-professed "member of the Harry Golden Fan Club."[75]

Humphrey and Golden began corresponding with one another while Humphrey was a Senator from Minnesota.[76] They also visited each other. Humphrey held Golden in such high esteem that he once wrote to Golden:

> Please let me know when you are going to be in Washington. There is so little time between the pressures of Congressional and constituent demands for friends. But, I would leave the floor at anytime to see you.[77]

The two men frequently exchanged opinions and ideas on the civil rights struggle.[78] On one such occasion, Humphrey informed Golden of his attempts to "provide federal voting registrars in areas where Negroes are denied the right to vote."[79] On another occasion, Humphrey commented to Golden, "Our dream of a better America is going to be fulfilled."[80] Humphrey also occasionally requested civil rights information and opinions from Golden, in addition to Golden's views expressed in the *Israelite*, for use in his political or governmental work. Subsequently, Golden provided Humphrey with civil rights background and research material for use in various Humphrey proposals and speeches.[81]

Golden's reputation as a journalistic civil rights advocate continued to live after the closing of the *Israelite* and led to the admiration of post-*Israelite* Presidents and members of their administrations. President Richard M. Nixon considered Golden a civil rights activist and "a man whose candor, courage, and compassion have exposed unquestioned fallacies in people's thinking and improved relations between black and white Americans."[82] Nixon's Vice President, Gerald R. Ford, was also a reader of the *Israelite* while he was a Congressman form Michigan.[83]

President Jimmy Carter was also familiar with Golden's advocacy. In addition, Carter's Vice President, Walter F. Mondale, considered Golden a friend and held him in high esteem.[84] Mondale once wrote to Golden:

> [F]or years I have admired you--not only for the warmth and joy of your writing, but even more for the values you have unashamedly affirmed throughout a lifetime of moral courage and social action.[85]

The Legislative Branch

Congress and Civil Rights. Congress provided support for the movement by enacting various civil rights legislation between 1957 and 1968. This legislation collectively brought blacks much closer to their goal of civil rights. The Civil Rights Act of 1957 was the first federal civil rights legislation enacted during the modern movement. The major provision of the Act was the establishment of a Commission on Civil Rights. The six-member Presidentially appointed commission was empowered to investigate and report on allegations of the denial of voting rights based on color, race, religion, or national origin. The 1957 Act also prohibited any person from interfering with another person's right to vote. In addition, the Act enabled the United States Attorney General to use preventive civil actions--injunctions, restraining orders--against people who were proved very likely to attempt to deprive others of their right to vote.[86]

With the Civil Rights Act of 1960, Congress responded to the rash of bombings that targeted members of the civil rights movement. The Act prohibited transporting, using, or possessing explosives for the purpose of interfering with the use of buildings or property for educational, religious, charitable, residential, business, or civic objectives. The Act also required that all records relating to voter registration applications be retained and preserved by election officials for 21 months. In addition, the 1960 Act provided for court-appointed voting referees who could determine if an individual was qualified to vote based on state requirements, including literacy testing. Congress enacted its most comprehensive civil rights legislation through the Civil Rights Act of 1964. It addressed voting rights in federal elections by requiring the criteria used to determine voter qualifications to be the same for all potential voters. The Act also restricted the use of literacy tests and prohibited denial of voting rights based on paperwork errors or omissions that were not material in determining an individual's qualifications. A major provision of the Act prohibited discrimination or segregation in public accommodations--hotels, restaurants, theaters--based on race, color, religion, or national origin.[87]

Another major provision of the Act prohibited employers from discriminating based on race, color, religion, sex, or national origin when hiring, promoting, and firing, or when selecting participants for job training programs. The same provision prohibited employment agencies and labor organizations from discriminating based on the aforementioned factors in job referrals and membership selection respectively. The Act also established an Equal Employment Opportunity Commission to furnish assistance to employers, employees, and potential employees concerning equal employment opportunity (EEO) laws.[88]

Congress enacted the Voting Rights Act of 1965 to provide additional and substantial support of black voting rights. The major provision of the Act included the prohibition of voter registration tests--reading, writing, interpretation--and poll taxes in all local, state, and federal elections. The Act also provided for court-appointed voting examiners who were empowered to screen and certify individuals as qualified voters based on state laws, providing those laws were not inconsistent with the U.S. Constitution and laws.[89] The Congress continued to expand legislative support of civil rights through the Civil Rights Act of 1968. A major provision of the Act outlawed discrimination based on race, color, religion, or national origin in the selling, renting, terms of selling or renting, and financing of real estate.[90]

Golden and Congress. Golden's journalistic civil rights advocacy was well known throughout the halls of the United States Senate and House of Representatives. The *Israelite* was read by numerous Senators and Representatives, both Democrats and Republicans. Golden also corresponded with members of the national legislature regularly. In addition, Golden's reputation as a civil rights advocate often led to the inclusion of *Israelite* editorials and comments about his advocacy in the *Congressional Record*. Golden was also occasionally requested to testify about civil rights before Senate and House committees.

Senate Interaction. Senator Edward Kennedy of Massachusetts, like his brothers President John F. Kennedy and Attorney General Robert F. Kennedy, was a reader of the *Israelite* and a friend of Golden.[91] Edward Kennedy believed that Golden was dedicated to "efforts on behalf of others."[92] Kennedy and Golden visited and often corresponded with one another concerning civil rights.[93] In one such correspondence, Kennedy informed Golden, "I agree with your belief that racism can be ended through compassion for our fellow man."[94]

Senator George McGovern of South Dakota was also a reader of the *Israelite*, a friend to Golden, and an "admirer" of Golden's journalistic talents.[95] According to McGovern, Golden had a "burning impatience with injustice"[96] which led him to fight for first-class citizenship of blacks. McGovern continued:

> [H]e [Golden] has helped to change our country, our Constitution, and our concept of social justice for the millions who have carried the burden of discrimination against their color. He has been. . . a worker in the struggle to make our land and our lives equal to our ideals.[97]

Other Senators also read the *Israelite* and held Golden in high esteem. Senator Thomas Kuchel of California considered Golden a "good man" and encouraged Golden to visit him in Washington.[98] Senator Edmund S. Muskie of Maine enjoyed reading the *Israelite* and considered Golden a man of "stature."[99] Muskie once wrote to Golden, "Your analysis of the problems of the American Negro especially interest me. I feel that there are obvious merits to your arguments."[100]

In addition, Golden and the *Israelite* had a geographically broad following in the Senate. Most of these Senators corresponded with Golden and considered him a friend. They included, but were not limited to: Gale McGee of Wyoming, Ernest Hollings of South Carolina, Ralph

Yarborough of Texas, Philip Hart of Michigan, Howard Baker of Tennessee, Frank Church of Idaho, William Fulbright of Arkansas, Claiborne Pell of Rhode Island, Ernest Gruening of Alaska, Joseph Clark and Hugh Scott of Pennsylvania, Eugene McCarthy of Minnesota, Thomas Dodd of Connecticut, Thomas Eagleton of Missouri, Vance Hartke of Indiana, and Jacob Javits of New York.[101]

Golden's reputation as a journalistic civil rights advocate and the esteem in which he was held by members of the Senate led to a formal request for his insight into race relations and the plight of blacks. In 1966, during a time of race riots,[102] Senator Abraham Ribicoff of Connecticut--Chairman of the Senate Subcommittee on Executive Reorganization of the Committee on Government Operations--requested Golden's "personal views on the crisis of the American city."[103] Ribicoff wrote to Golden, "We believe you can make a significant contribution to the understanding of urban problems."[104] Golden readily accepted the invitation[105] and took the opportunity to provide the Subcommittee with his perspective on the plight of many blacks in urban settings.

Golden informed the Subcommittee that America had "wronged the Negro."[106] According to Golden, many blacks were hopelessly trapped in urban ghettoes. He argued that political, educational, social, and economic discrimination had locked them in. He also pointed out racism as the root of such discrimination. Golden commented that cities across America rested on "smoldering volcanoes" because of the frustration and hopelessness caused by racism.[107] He suggested that the federal government fight poverty and ensure black civil rights in order to remedy the situation.[108] He also recommended a cooperative effort between the government and business sectors in providing educational employment opportunity for blacks. He contended that such a cooperation could "break down the walls of the ghettoes."[109]

Golden's journalistic advocacy and the admiration of members of the Senate also led to the inclusion of information about Harry Golden in the *Congressional Record* on several occasions. In June of 1964, Senator Harrison Williams of New Jersey entered the following comments about Golden in the *Record*:

> [O]ur most pressing social problems usually become less pressing when we establish even basic communication among those who are in disagreement.[110]
>
> Harry Golden is one of those in our Nation today who is trying to increase communication in the struggle to give full citizenship to all of our citizens.[111]

In October of 1964, Senator Philip Hart of Michigan also entered comments about Golden in the *Record*:

> Harry Golden discusses the subjects of race and immigration in the interesting perspective fashion which is his and which has influenced, for good, many of the public debates and decisions in this country. He treats the subject in a most unusual but penetrating way.[112]

Hart entered additional comments about Golden in the *Record* during February of 1965. He encouraged his colleagues to read Golden, commenting:

> [I]n the weeks and months ahead we shall discuss and debate in this chamber the role which the Federal Government should play in broadening educational opportunities for all Americans. I hope all Senators will have an opportunity to read the brief and vivid comment

> recently penned by a distinguished citizen of North Carolina, Harry Golden.[113]
>
> [H]e has described, effectively, the place education must hold if our society is to become the great one which each of us prays it will.[114]

Hart then entered Golden's statement on the "War on Poverty" into the *Record.* Golden's comments reflected his commitment to black civil rights and stressed "the poverty of the Negro" was "acute" and education was "the only answer."[115] Golden's advocacy and relationship with members of the Senate not only promoted thought and discussion about civil rights, it also fostered concern among some Senators about Golden's well-being. Senator James Murray of Montana illustrated this concern for Golden and his journalistic civil rights advocacy when part of Golden's *Israelite* offices were destroyed by fire.[116] During that time Murray entered news of the fire and his opinion of Golden in the *Record*:

> One of the most remarkable journalists in the land is Mr. Harry Golden, who publishes the *Carolina Israelite* in Charlotte, N.C. Mr. Golden is a learned man with a sense of humor. He has the ability to make Americans think and, at the same time, chuckle. Unfortunately, a fire recently destroyed his office, vast collection of books and personal treasures, and a portion of his subscription list. But fortunately, the *Carolina Israelite* will continue publication.[117]

***House of Representatives Interaction*.** Golden's journalistic civil rights advocacy also led to his recognition by members of the House. As with the Senate, Golden made friends with many Representatives and corresponded with them concerning civil rights. For example, Representative Charles Jonas of North Carolina was a reader of the *Israelite* and shared a "cordial friendship" with Golden.[118] He admired Golden's approach to civil rights advocacy. According to Jonas:

> Harry's voice was always a quiet one. And it was a voice spiced with humor. Who will forget the days of bitter controversy when there suddenly burst upon the scene the Golden plan of vertical integration?[119]

Other Representatives also appreciated Golden's advocacy. Donald Fraser of Minnesota found Golden's insight into segregation valuable.[120] Barrat O'Hara of Illinois "appreciated the *Israelite* and received a great deal of enjoyment while reading it."[121] A.W. Joslyn of Idaho wrote Golden, "Your newspaper is very good and I am enclosing a check for a subscription."[122] Nick Galifianakis of North Carolina wrote, "I have always been an admirer of yours."[123]

In addition, the *Israelite* was read by a broad cross section of Representatives, most of whom corresponded with Golden. Among others, they included: Seymour Halpern, Leonard Farbstein, Steven Derounian, Emanuel Celler, Herbert Zelenko, Edward Koch, and Elizabeth Holtzman of New York; James Broyhill, Earl Ruth, Roy Taylor, and Horace Kornegay of North Carolina; Robert Drinan and Michael Harrington of Massachusetts; Melvin Laird of Wisconsin; Rogers Morton of Maryland; Clark MacGregor of Minnesota; John Culver of Iowa; and William Anderson of Tennessee.[124]

As with the Senate, Golden's reputation as a journalistic civil rights advocate, as well as the esteem held for Golden by the members of the House,[125] led to a formal request for the sharing of his insight to a House Subcommittee. Although the *Israelite* had been closed for four years, in 1972 Golden was asked to comment on busing and school integration before the House Committee on the Judiciary.[126] Among Golden's comments he noted:

> [B]using is not the issue at all. Segregation is the issue. Busing is a fact of life. . . . For years hundreds of Negro pupils were bussed past the white schools to their segregated Negro schools and no one protested. So the issue is not whether pupils would be bussed but which schools they would attend. . . . The interesting aspect about busing is that folks who are against it always start their argument with, "I am not a racist, but. . ." The simple truth is that they do not want their children in school with black children. . . . What is the solution? Law is the solution! The South has overcome much more volatile controversies than busing. . . . Law did it. . . . Law doesn't change the hearts of men, but it changes their practices. Morals follow the Law.[127]

Representative Ogden Reid of New York later wrote to Golden, "Your statement before the Committee on the Judiciary was just excellent."[128]

As was the case in the Senate, Golden's advocacy and the admiration of members of the House led to the inclusion of his opinions in the *Congressional Record* on several occasions. On one such occasion an *Israelite* reader, Representative Charles Diggs of Michigan, entered the complete text of Golden's Out-of-Order Plan[129] in the *Record*.[130] Later, when the Out-of-Order Plan was actually utilized in North Carolina[131] another *Israelite* reader, Representative James Roosevelt of California, entered a discussion of such use in the *Record*:

> Mr. Harry Golden's solutions to some of the problems of the South are not unknown to many of my colleagues. As editor and publisher of the Carolina Israelite, Mr. Golden has his own unique forum for the presentation of such schemes as his Out-of-Order Plan.[132]

Roosevelt also entered the text of an *Israelite* article, describing the use of the plan, in the *Record.*[133]

Diggs was also responsible for entering Golden's White Baby Plan[134] in the *Record.* Prior to placing the plan in the *Record*, Diggs commented on the significance of Golden's satire:

> Mr. Golden's humorous yet pointed remarks illustrate clearly the ludicrous conclusions which can be reached by founding arguments on the false premise of racial superiority.[135]

Representative Charles Weltner of Georgia entered a letter from Golden in the *Record.*[136] In the letter Golden expressed his views on the unfulfillment of the "American Dream" for blacks. Golden wrote to Weltner:

> [T]he American dream is the opportunity of entering the open society. . . . There are twenty-four million "strangers" wanting in to the open society. . . . These twenty-four million "strangers" have curiously lived in America longer than most of the population. . . . These strangers are the American Negroes.[137]

The appeal of Golden and his journalistic civil rights advocacy led to admiration by the leaders of the Judicial, Executive, and Legislative branches of the federal government. In addition, his advocacy was also appealing to members of other federal government segments. The following section discusses Golden's appeal to such segments.

Other Segments of Government

Golden was also read and admired by officials of numerous and varied other segments--departments, agencies, commissions--of the federal government. Federal Communications Commission Chairman Newton Minow read the *Israelite*, corresponded with Golden, and considered him a friend.[138] On one occasion Minow wrote to Golden, "Your current issue [of the *Israelite*] is again a delight."[139]

John Buggs, Staff Director of the U.S. Commission on Civil Rights, also held Golden in high esteem. He considered Golden a "prominent"[140] civil rights advocate. As a result, Buggs selected Golden as a person whose "experiences, perceptions, and opinions" would be of "utmost value"[141] in the Commission's twenty-year assessment of the impact of *Brown v. Board of Education*[142] on "the entire field of civil rights."[143] Golden also corresponded with officials in numerous other segments of the government including the Department of Commerce, Department of Health Education and Welfare, Department of State, and the Department of Justice. In addition, he maintained contact with the U.S. Information Agency.[144]

Institutional Recognition

Golden and the *Israelite* appealed to a broad cross section of the American public--young and old, black and white, Jews and gentiles, southerners and northerners.[145] At one point in the late 1950s, the paper reached over 50,000 readers in 49 American states and 33 foreign countries.[146] Some of Golden's readers even formed a Harry Golden Fan Club.[147] His civil rights advocacy was also praised by a variety of segments and institutions in American society. The following examination of the numerous awards and honors received by Golden illustrates the esteem in which he was held.

Educational Honors

Golden received honorary doctoral degrees from a diverse group of colleges because of his work as a humanitarian. Belmont Abbey College, a Catholic institution, presented Golden with such a degree in 1962. In 1965, Johnson C. Smith University, a predominantly black institution, presented Golden with an honorary doctorate. Thiel College, a Lutheran institution, presented Golden with a doctoral degree in 1974. In addition, the University of North Carolina at Charlotte, a predominantly white institution, presented Golden with a doctorate in 1977.[148]

Golden also received other honors from colleges and universities. In 1955, Carver College, a predominantly black institution, honored Golden by awarding him a citation for improving race relations in the South. The University of North Carolina at Charlotte honored Golden by declaring

May 7, 1969 as Harry Golden Day. The university sought to praise Golden for his scholarship and social conscience.[149] According to the proclamation:

> [H]e [Golden] made us face vexing and explosive problems, he also helped us find the humor in them and has persuaded us that reconciliation is ultimately possible.[150]

The university also established a Harry Golden lectureship as a tribute to Golden. The lectureship was designed to serve as a permanent series of presentations on Golden's career and interests.[151]

In 1983, Golden received posthumous praise for his civil rights advocacy from the University of North Carolina a Chapel Hill. At that time, the University's School of Journalism inducted Golden into the North Carolina Journalism Hall of Fame.[152] He was cited for his civil rights advocacy through the *Israelite*.[153]

Black Organizational Honors

Several black organizations--professional, fraternal, civic--honored Golden for his journalistic civil rights advocacy. In 1958, the National Newspaper Publishers Association honored Golden with its Russwurm Award. The award was named for John B. Russwurm, one of the founding editors of *Freedom's Journal*, the first black-published newspaper in the United States. Golden was recognized for promoting American ideals and democratic principles.[154]

Golden received another award named after a distinguished journalistic advocate of racial equality in 1964. At that time, the Elks Grand Lodge presented him with their Lovejoy Award. The award was named for Elijah Parish Lovejoy, a journalist who published an anti-slavery publication--the *Observer*--during the 1830s. Lovejoy was murdered by a mob and his press was destroyed because of his abolitionist views. Golden's acceptance of the award for civil rights advocacy placed him in the company of previous noteworthy recipients such as Martin Luther King, Jr., A. Phillip Randolph, Roy Wilkins, and Thurgood Marshall.[155]

The Omega Psi Phi fraternity also presented Golden with an award during the 1960s. The fraternity cited Golden for fighting "unyieldingly, uncompromisingly, unabashed, even against the odds" in the battle for "first class citizenship for all people."[156] Golden's civil rights advocacy was also celebrated by blacks after his death. This is exemplified by Golden's posthumous induction into the NAACP Hall of Fame in 1986.[157] He was praised for his "unchallenged commitment to human and civil rights"[158] and for "dedicating his life to exposing the hypocrisy of segregation and racism in America."[159]

Jewish Organizational Honors

Several Jewish organizations also celebrated Golden's advocacy and humanitarianism. In 1959, he was designated Man of the Year by the National Federation of Temple Brotherhoods. Golden was praised for his "significant contributions to the American ideals of equality and justice to people of all races and creeds."[160]

During the same year, Golden was proclaimed Man of the Year by Agudas and Beth Israel Brotherhoods. He was credited for "Humanitarian interests on behalf of his fellowmen without regard to race, creed, or color."[161] Golden also received an award for "Distinguished Journalism" in 1959 from the American Jewish Committee-Anti Defamation League.[162] In addition, he received the Grand Master Award of the Brith Abraham organization for his "fight against injustice."[163] The 1960 award cited Golden for upholding the dignity of man and aiding the less fortunate.[164]

Southern and Northern Honors

Golden's advocacy brought him acclaim from the South and the North, as exemplified by the following. In 1957, Governor Luther Hodges of North Carolina awarded Golden the title of Ambassador of Goodwill for North Carolina. By 1979, Governor James Hunt of North Carolina awarded Golden the North Carolina Award in Literature, the state's highest honor for a writer. Golden was recognized for improving the lives of people everywhere by using his journalism to reduce injustice and support humanitarian causes.[165]

Golden's journalistic advocacy was also appreciated in the North. Upon his death in 1981, the City Council of Chicago, Illinois adopted a resolution in his honor. The City Council proclaimed Golden an "anti-racist crusader." They praised him for his efforts on behalf of civil rights and equality and expressed regret at his death.[166]

Other Honors

Golden's advocacy was also acclaimed by a variety of other organizations representing different segments of America. For example, in 1959, one of Golden's childhood schools--Public School 20 in New York City--presented him with a citation. The school recognized him for "carrying the torch to light the way to an America truly united without regard to race, color, religion, or national origin."[167] Another example of the diversity among groups honoring Golden's advocacy and humanitarianism was an award from the Old North State Medical Society. In 1965, the society recognized Golden for "exceptional contributions to human relations."[168]

Praise for Golden's civil rights advocacy also took a different form from awards. Golden was held in high esteem by many authors who wrote about the civil rights movement. Subsequently, he has been cited in numerous such publications. For example, Thomas R. Brooks, in *Walls Come Tumbling Down: A History of the Civil Rights Movement*, refers to Golden's Vertical Negro and Out-of-Order Plans to illustrate the "ludicrous Patchwork" of segregation.[169]

Similarly, Robert Penn Warren in *Who Speaks for the Negro* refers to Golden in an analysis of "the people who are making the Negro revolution what it is."[170] Bradford Daniels, in *Black, White, and Gray: Twenty One Points of View on the Race Question* also includes Golden's views on civil rights.[171] In addition, Taylor Branch in *Parting the Waters: America in the King Years 1954-1963*[172] and Calder Pickett in *Voices of the Past: Key Documents in the History of American Journalism*[173] both cite works of Golden. Golden's friends and fellow journalistic civil rights advocates, Harry Ashmore and Ralph McGill, also included comments about Golden's advocacy in their books *Hearts and Minds* and *No Place to Hide: The South and Human Rights*, respectively.[174]

Many and varied segments of the American public were familiar with, and positively influenced by, Golden's advocacy. His work was highly praised. His journalistic civil rights advocacy was appealing to his broad readership (including influential citizens--government and civil rights leaders).

Chapter Three Notes

[1]See Appendix A for a discussion of the SCLC and CORE.

[2]C.T. Vivian, letter to Harry Golden, 8 Oct. 1964, Box 9 File 5, Harry Golden Collection Part II, U of North Carolina at Charlotte; James Farmer, letter to Harry Golden, 9 July 1962, Box 19 File 30, Harry Golden Collection Part II, U of North Carolina at Charlotte.

[3]Wyatt Tee Walker, letter to Harry Golden, 2 July 1962, Box 32 File 686, Harry Golden Collection Part I, U of North Carolina at Charlotte; Wyatt Tee Walker, letter to Harry Golden, 6 Nov. 1963, Box 19 File 5, Harry Golden Collection Part II, U of North Carolina at Charlotte.

[4]Vivian, letter to Harry Golden, 8 Oct. 1964.

[5]Edward King, letter to Harry Golden, 13 April 1961, Box 19 File 30, Harry Golden Collection Part II, U of North Carolina at Charlotte. Golden resigned from SNCC in 1967, after the organization's leadership began to support black militancy. Golden believed that the new direction of SNCC was anti-semitic and made a "mockery" of nonviolence. See Harry Golden, letter to Rolfe Featherstone, 18 Aug. 1967, Box 9 File 30, Harry Golden Collection Part II, U of North Carolina at Charlotte; See Appendix A for a discussion of

SNCC; Mildred Bond, letters to Harry Golden, May 1959 and 8 Sept. 1960, Box 14 File 1, Harry Golden Collection Part II, U of North Carolina at Charlotte; Roy Wilkins, letters to Harry Golden, 6 Feb. 1961 and 11 May 1963, Box 14 File 1, Harry Golden Collection Part II, U of North Carolina at Charlotte.

[6]Edward King, letter to Harry Golden, 13 April 1961; Harry Golden, "1312 Elizabeth Avenue," *Carolina Israelite* Sept./Oct. 1962: 6; Ralph Bunche, letters to Harry Golden, 18 Mar. 1964 and 30 Mar. 1964, Box 14 File 1, Harry Golden Collection Part II, U of North Carolina at Charlotte; Alfred Baker Lewis, letter to Harry Golden, 14 Feb. 1962, Box 14 File 1, Harry Golden Collection Part II, U of North Carolina at Charlotte; Kelly M. Alexander, letter to Harry Golden, 26 Sept. 1960, Box 14 File 1, Harry Golden Collection Part II, U of North Carolina at Charlotte; Harry Golden, "An Hysterical Audience," the *Carolina Israelite* Jan./Feb. 1962: 12; Harry Golden, *Harry Golden Remembers* Vanguard, VRS-9102, 1958. See Appendix A for a discussion of the NAACP.

[7]See the discussion of Golden and civil rights organizations in this chapter. A. Phillip Randolph, letter to Harry Golden, July 1966, Box 17 File 10, Harry Golden Collection Part II, U of North Carolina at Charlotte. See Executive Branch in the Governmental Leaders section of this chapter for information on the White House Civil Rights Conference; A. Phillip Randolph, letter to Harry Golden, 28 Aug. 1970, Box 17 File 10, Harry Golden Collection Part II, U of North Carolina at Charlotte; Harry Golden, letter to A. Phillip Randolph, 1 Sept. 1979, Box 17 File 10, Harry Golden Collection Part II, U of North Carolina at Charlotte.

[8]A. Phillip Randolph, letter to Harry Golden, 10 Sept. 1963, Box 17 File 10, Harry Golden Collection Part II, U of North Carolina at Charlotte; Harry Golden, letter to A. Phillip Randolph, 24 Sept. 1963, Box 17 File 10, Harry Golden Collection Part II, U of North Carolina at Charlotte.

[9]Roy Wilkins, letter to George Abernathy, 16 June 1969, Box 14 File 1, Harry Golden Collection Part II, U of North Carolina at Charlotte; Roy Wilkins, letter to Harry Golden, 13 May 1964, Harry Golden Collection Part II, U of North Carolina at Charlotte.

[10]Roy Wilkins, "statement" for Harry Golden Day, 19 May 1969, Box 2 File 37, Harry Golden Collection Part II, U of North Carolina at Charlotte.

[11]See Appendix A and Chapter 3 for a discussion of Dr. Martin Luther King, Jr.

[12]Wyatt Tee Walker, letter to Harry Golden, 4 May 1964, Box 9 File 5, Harry Golden Collection Part II, U of North Carolina at Charlotte.

[13]Martin Luther King, Jr., letter to Harry Golden, 30 April 1964, Box 11 File 29, Harry Golden Collection Part II, U of North Carolina at Charlotte. See Appendix A for a discussion of the Birmingham campaign and Children's Crusade.

[14]The Alabama clergymen were: C. Carpenter, the Catholic Bishop of Alabama; Joseph Durick, the Catholic Auxiliary Bishop of Mobile; Milton Grafman, a Birmingham Rabbi; Paul Hardin, a Methodist Bishop; Nolan Harmon, a Methodist Bishop; George Murray, an Episcopal Bishop; Edward Ramage, a Presbyterian Moderator; and Earl Stallings, a Baptist Pastor. See Martin Luther King, Jr., *Letter from Birmingham City Jail* (Birmingham: American Friends Service Committee, 1963) 15.

[15]King, *Letter from Birmingham City Jail* 3, 8.

[16]King, *Letter from Birmingham City Jail* 8.

[17]King, *Letter from Birmingham City Jail* 5.

[18]King, *Letter from Birmingham City Jail* 5, 6.

[19]King, *Letter form Birmingham City Jail* 11.

[20]King, *Letter from Birmingham City Jail* 11. See Appendix B for a discussion of Ralph McGill. Lillian Smith was a civil rights advocate and author. Included among her books are *Killers of the Dream* (New York: Norton, 1949), and

Now is the Time (New York: Viking, 1955). She also wrote for the *Atlanta Constitution*. James Dabbs was also a civil rights advocate and author. Included among his books are *Southern Heritage* (New York: Knopf, 1958), and *Haunted by God* (Richmond: Knox, 1972).

[21]King, *Letter from Birmingham City Jail* 11.

[22]Martin Luther King, Jr., letter to Harry Golden, 3 Nov. 1964, Box 19 File 5, Harry Golden Collection Part II, U of North Carolina at Charlotte; Martin Luther King, Jr., letter to Harry Golden, 15 Nov. 1965, Box 19 File 5, Harry Golden Collection Part II, U of North Carolina at Charlotte.

[23]King, letter to Harry Golden, 15 Nov. 1965; Harry Golden, letter to Martin Luther King, Jr., 17 Nov. 1965, Box 11 File 29, Harry Golden Collection Part II, U of North Carolina at Charlotte; Harry Wachtel, memorandum to American Foundation on Nonviolence Board of Directors, 26 April 1966, Box 11 File 29, Harry Golden Collection Part II, U of North Carolina at Charlotte. By July 26, 1966 the Board of Directors had used some of the funds for voter education and registration grants in Alabama, Mississippi, and Georgia. See "minutes" of the AFON Board of Directors, 26 July 1966, Box 11 File 29, Harry Golden Collection Part II, U of North Carolina at Charlotte.

[24]Martin Luther King, Jr., letter to Harry Golden, 2 July 1962, Box 19 File 5, Harry Golden Collection Part II, U of North Carolina at Charlotte; Harry Golden, telegram to Martin Luther King, Jr., 15 Oct. 1964, Box 19 File 5, Harry Golden Collection Part II, U of North Carolina at Charlotte; Martin Luther King, Jr., telegram to Harry Golden, 18 Mar. 1965, Box 11 File 19, Harry Golden Collection Part II, U of North Carolina at Charlotte; Harry Golden, telegram to Martin Luther King, Jr., 18 Mar. 1965, Box 11 File 29, Harry Golden Collection Part II, U of North Carolina at Charlotte; Martin Luther King, Jr., telegram to Harry Golden, 7 July 1966, Box 11 File 29, Harry Golden Collection Part II, U of North

Carolina at Charlotte. See Appendix A for a discussion of martyrs of the civil rights movement.

[25]Harry Golden, *So Long as You're Healthy* (New York: Putnam, 1970) 230.

[26]Golden, *So Long as You're Healthy* 230.

[27]Julian Bond, personal interview, 7 Sept. 1994.

[28]John Lewis, personal interview, 25 July 1994.

[29]Andrew Young, personal interview, 10 Aug. 1994.

[30]C. T. Vivian, personal interview, 12 Aug. 1994.

[31]James Farmer, personal interview, 6 Jan. 1996.

[32]Harry Golden, *The Right Time: An Autobiography, by Harry Golden* (New York: Putnam, 1969) 252. See Chapter 2 for a discussion of Golden's use of the *Israelite*.

[33]See Appendix A for a discussion of major civil rights leaders and organizations.

[34]*Brown v. Board of Education of Topeka, Kansas, 74 S. Ct. 686; 347 U.S. 483, 1954. See Appendix A for a discussion of this case.*

[35]See Appendix A for a discussion of the Montgomery bus boycott.

[36]*Browder v. Gayle* 352 U.S. 903; 202 F. Supp. 707, 1956.

[37]Ralph David Abernathy, *And the Walls Came Tumbling Down* (New York: Harper and Row, 1989) 175, 190.

[38]The *Israelite* was also read by lower level judges such as J. Braxton Craven, Jr. of the U.S. Fourth Judicial Circuit. Braxton corresponded with Golden and considered Golden to be his friend. See J. Braxton Craven, Jr., letter to Robert Wallace, 12 April 1971, Box 2 File 28, Harry Golden Collection Part II, U of North Carolina at Charlotte. See Earl Warren, correspondence with Harry Golden, 1961, Box 21 File 2, Harry Golden Collection Part II, U of North Carolina at Charlotte; "Golden Rule," *Time* 1 April 1957: 62. Felix Frankfurter, letter to Harry Golden, 1 July 1959, Box 32 File 686, Harry Golden Collection Part II, U of North Carolina at Charlotte; Harry Golden, "Goodbye," the *Carolina Israelite*

Jan./Feb. 1968: 2. Arthur Goldberg, letter to Harry Golden, 14 May 1964, Box 7 File 52, Harry Golden Collection Part II, U of North Carolina at Charlotte; Harry Golden, letter to Arthur Goldberg, 10 Sept. 1962, Box 7 File 52, Harry Golden Collection Part II, U of North Carolina at Charlotte.

[39]Hugo Black, letter to Harry Golden, 18 Dec. 1968, Box 3 File 27, Harry Golden Collection Part II, U of North Carolina at Charlotte; Hugo Black, letter to Harry Golden, 1 July 1963, Box 3 File 27, Harry Golden Collection Part II, U of North Carolina at Charlotte.

[40]Hugo Black, letter to Harry Golden, 5 Mar. 1970, Box 3 File 27, Harry Golden Collection Part II, U of North Carolina at Charlotte.

[41]See Chapter 2 for a brief discussion of Golden's health at the time the *Israelite* closed.

[42]Hugo Black, letter to Harry Golden, 11 Dec. 1968, Box 3 File 27, Harry Golden Collection Part II, U of North Carolina at Charlotte.

[43]Hugo Black, letter to Harry Golden, 26 Oct. 1970, Box 3 File 27, Harry Golden Collection Part II, U of North Carolina at Charlotte.

[44]Black, letter to Harry Golden, 26 Oct. 1970.

[45]William O. Douglas, foreword, *The Best of Harry Golden*, by Harry Golden (Cleveland: World, 1967) ix.

[46]William O. Douglas, *Go East, Young Man* (New York: Vintage, 1974) 345.

[47]Douglas, Foreword ix.

[48]William O. Douglas, letter to Harry Golden, 1 Mar. 1968, Box 6 File 18, Harry Golden Collection Part II, U of North Carolina at Charlotte.

[49]Douglas, foreword ix.

[50]Harry Golden, letter to William O. Douglas, 11 Nov. 1974, Harry Golden Collection Part II, U of North Carolina at Charlotte.

[51]See Appendix A for discussions of the "Little Rock Nine," the Birmingham campaign, and "Bloody Sunday" and the Selma to Montgomery march. Juan Williams, *Eyes on the Prize* (New York: Penguin, 1988) 195, 217-217, 279. "Troops are Sent to Alabama Bases in Wake of Birmingham Rioting," *Atlanta Constitution* 13 May 1963: 1; Williams 194.

[52]Harry Golden, *Mr. Kennedy and the Negroes* (Cleveland: World, 1964) 140, 143, 150.

[53]Williams 195.

[54]See the discussion of the Civil Rights Act of 1964 later in this section.

[55]See the discussion of the Voting Rights Act of 1965 later in this section.

[56]Lyndon B. Johnson, "The American Promise," *Congressional Record* Senate, 89th Cong., 1st sess., (Washington, D.C.: U.S. Government Printing Office, 1965) 22517.

[57]Harry Golden, letter to Harry Truman, 17 Feb. 1965, Box 19 File 64, Harry Golden Collection Part II, U of North Carolina at Charlotte; Harry Truman, letter to Harry Golden, 9 Mar. 1965, Box 19 File 64, Harry Golden Collection Part II, U of North Carolina at Charlotte. Dwight Eisenhower, letter to Harry Golden, 4 Dec. 1946, Box 6 File 35, Harry Golden Collection Part II, U of North Carolina at Charlotte. Golden also corresponded with the wives of Presidents, such as Jacqueline Kennedy and Eleanor Roosevelt. Jacqueline Kennedy, letter to Harry Golden, 19 Jan. 1965, Harry Golden Collection, William Goldhurst Private Holdings, Gainesville; Eleanor Roosevelt, letters to Harry Golden, 30 June 1960 and 27 Mar. 1962, Box 17 File 31, Harry Golden Collection Part II, U of North Carolina at Charlotte.

[58]Edward Kennedy, telegram to E.W. Colvard, 19 May 1969, Box 2 File 37, Harry Golden Collection Part II, U of North Carolina at Charlotte. Golden first met John and Robert Kennedy in 1957. All were participating in a Boston conference on retarded children. Their respective families each

had a retarded child. See Harry Golden, *The Right Time: An Autobiography, by Harry Golden* (New York: Putnam, 1969) 414.

[59]John F. Kennedy, letters to Harry Golden, 13 Mar. 1959 and 29 July 1959, Box 32 File 283, Harry Golden Collection Part I, U of North Carolina at Charlotte; John F. Kennedy, letter to Harry Golden, 17 Dec. 1960, Box 11 File 11, Harry Golden Collection Part II, U of North Carolina at Charlotte; Golden, *The Right Time* 429.

[60]Golden, *The Right Time* 417.

[61]Golden, *The Right Time* 426.

[62]John F. Kennedy, letter to Harry Golden, 20 Aug. 1960, Box 32 File 283, Harry Golden Collection Part I, U of North Carolina at Charlotte; Golden, *The Right Time* 317.

[63]John F. Kennedy, invitation to Harry Golden, June 1966, Box 10 File 37, Harry Golden Collection Part II, U of North Carolina at Charlotte; Ben Heineman, letter to Harry Golden, 14 May 1966, Box 10 File 37, Harry Golden Collection Part II, U of North Carolina at Charlotte.

[64]*White House Conference: "To Fulfill These Rights"* (Washington, D.C.: The White House, 1966) 1-2, 41.

[65]Golden, *The Right Time* 431.

[66]Robert F. Kennedy, letters to Harry Golden, 6 Nov. 1959, 22 June 1960, 29 July 1963, and 14 Aug. 1963, Box 11 File 17, Harry Golden Collection Part II, U of North Carolina at Charlotte; Golden, *The Right Time* 436; Harry Golden, *Ess, Ess Mein Kindt* (New York: Putnam 1966) 256.

[67]Robert F. Kennedy, letters to Harry Golden, 27 March 1959, Box 11 File 7, Harry Golden Collection Part II, U of North Carolina at Charlotte.

[68]Golden, *Ess, Ess Mein Kindt* 257.

[69]Golden, *Ess, Ess Mein Kindt* 257.

[70]Lyndon B. Johnson, letters to Harry Golden, 2 Sept. 1960 and 15 June 1968, Box 10 File 37, Harry Golden Collection Part II, U of North Carolina at Charlotte; Lyndon B.

Johnson, letter to Harry Golden, 19 Aug. 1964, Box 10 File 38, Harry Golden Collection Part II, U of North Carolina at Charlotte.

[71]Harry Golden, memorandum to Lyndon B. Johnson, p. 3-4, Sept. 1964, Harry Golden Collection, William Goldhurst Private Holdings, Gainesville.

[72]Harry Golden, memorandum to Lyndon B. Johnson, p. 1.

[73]Lyndon B. Johnson, letter to Harry Golden, 29 Dec. 1964, Box 10 File 37, Harry Golden Collection Part II, U of North Carolina at Charlotte.

[74]Hubert H. Humphrey, letter to Harry Golden, 23 Aug. 1968, Box 9 File 9, Harry Golden Collection Part II, U of North Carolina at Charlotte.

[75]Hubert H. Humphrey, letter to Harry Golden, 30 June 1966, Box 9 File 9, Harry Golden Collection Part II, U of North Carolina at Charlotte.

[76]Hubert H. Humphrey, letter to Harry Golden, 21 Jan. 1960, Box 9 File 9, Harry Golden Collection Part II, U of North Carolina at Charlotte.

[77]Hubert H. Humphrey, letter to Harry Golden, 5 June 1962, Box 9 File 9, Harry Golden Collection Part II, U of North Carolina at Charlotte.

[78]Hubert H. Humphrey, letters to Harry Golden, 5 June 1962, 4 Sept. 1964, and 30 Aug. 1966, Box 9 File 9, Harry Golden Collection Part II, U of North Carolina at Charlotte.

[79]Hubert H. Humphrey, letter to Harry Golden, 21 Jan. 1960, Box 9 File 9, Harry Golden Collection Part II, U of North Carolina at Charlotte.

[80]Hubert H. Humphrey, letter to Harry Golden, 4 Sept. 1964, Box 9 File 9, Harry Golden Collection Part II, U of North Carolina at Charlotte.

[81]Hubert H. Humphrey, letter to Harry Golden, 10 Sept. 1964, Box 10 File 38, Harry Golden Collection Part II, U of North Carolina at Charlotte. Harry Golden, letter to Hubert H. Humphrey, 24 Mar. 1964, Harry Golden Collection Part II, U of North Carolina at Charlotte.

[82]Richard M. Nixon, telegram to Harry Golden, 18 May 1969, Box 2 File 37, Harry Golden Collection Part II, U of North Carolina at Charlotte; Richard M. Nixon, letter to Harry Golden, 3 Nov. 1972, Harry Golden Collection Part II, U of North Carolina at Charlotte.

[83]Gerald R. Ford, letter to Harry Golden, 19 Aug. 1965, Box 7 File 23, Harry Golden Collection Part II, U of North Carolina at Charlotte.

[84]Jimmy Carter, note to Harry Golden, Mar. 1977, Box 4 File 22, Harry Golden Collection Part II, U of North Carolina at Charlotte; Lloyd Corwin, letter to Harry Golden, 12 Jan. 1977, Box 4 File 22, Harry Golden Collection Part II, U of North Carolina at Charlotte. Walter F. Mondale, letter to Harry Golden, 29 July 1976, Harry Golden Collection Part II, U of North Carolina at Charlotte.

[85]Walter F. Mondale, letter to Harry Golden, 10 April 1980, Box 13 File 43, Harry Golden Collection Part II, U of North Carolina at Charlotte.

[86]Prior to the 1957 Act, Congress enacted the Civil Rights Act of 1875. The Act guaranteed all Americans the right to public accommodations. However, the law did not make segregated accommodations illegal. United States, 44th Congress, "Civil Rights Act of 1875," *United States Statutes at Large* (Washington, D.C.: GPO, 1875) 335. United States, 85th Congress, "Civil Rights Act of 1957," *United States Statutes at Large* (Washington, D.C.: GPO, 1958) 634-635, 637.

[87]See Appendix A for information on bombings and violence against civil rights workers. United States, 86th Congress, "Civil Rights Act of 1960," *United States Statutes at Large* Washington, D.C.: GPO, 1961) 86-88, 90-91, 206; Alphonso Pinkney, *The Committed* (New Haven: College and University, 1968) 206. Only written tests could be used. After the test a copy of the questions and answers had to be made available to the applicant. United States, 88th Congress, "Civil Rights Act of 1964," *United States Statutes at Large*

(Washington, D.C.: GPO, 1965) 241, 243-244; Gus Solomon, *The Jewish Role in the American Civil Rights Movement* (London: Jewish World Congress, 1967) 13, 15-16.

[88]88th Congress, "Civil Rights Act of 1964" 253, 255-256.

[89]United States, 89th Congress, "Voting Rights Act of 1965," *United States Statutes at Large* Washington, D.C.: GPO, 1966) 438, 440-442; Harry Golden, "The President's Voting Proposals," the *Carolina Israelite* Mar./April 1965: 7. 89th Congress, "Voting Rights Act of 1965" 440.

[90]United States, 90th Congress, "Civil Rights Act of 1968," *United States Statutes at Large* (Washington, D.C.: GPO, 1969) 83; Paul Horton, *The Sociology of Social Problems* 5th ed. (Englewood Cliffs: Prentice-Hall, 1974) 421.

[91]Edward Kennedy, telegram to E.W. Colvard, 19 May 1969, Box 2 File 37, Harry Golden Collection Part II, U of North Carolina at Charlotte.

[92]Edward Kennedy, telegram to Harry Golden, 21 Nov. 1966, Box 11 File 24, Harry Golden Collection Part II, U of North Carolina at Charlotte.

[93]Edward Kennedy, letters to Harry Golden, 4 Jan. 1967, 23 Sept. 1968, 9 Dec. 1971, 20 Mar. 1973, 16 Oct. 1974, Box 11 File 24, Harry Golden Collection Part II, U of North Carolina at Charlotte.

[94]Edward Kennedy, letter to Harry Golden, 6 Mar. 1970, Box 11 File 24, Harry Golden Collection Part II, U of North Carolina at Charlotte.

[95]George McGovern, letter to Harry Golden, 12 Aug. 1972, Box 13 File 51, Harry Golden Collection Part II, U of North Carolina at Charlotte; George McGovern, letter to William Goldhurst, 18 Feb. 1983, Harry Golden Collection, William Goldhurst Private Holdings, Gainesville; George McGovern, letter to Harry Golden, 23 Aug. 1972, Box 13 File 21, Harry Golden Collection Part II, U of North Carolina at Charlotte.

[96]George McGovern, "remarks" for Harry Golden Day at the U of North Carolina at Charlotte, 9 April 1973, Harry Golden Collection, William Goldhurst Private Holdings, Gainesville.

[97]George McGovern, "remarks" for Harry Golden Day.

[98]Thomas Kuchel, letter to Harry Golden, 3 Mar. 1965, Box 20 File 18, Harry Golden Collection Part II, U of North Carolina at Charlotte.

[99]Edmund Muskie, letter to Harry Golden, Mar. 1971, Box 13 File 51, Harry Golden Collection Part II, U of North Carolina at Charlotte.

[100]Edmund Muskie, letter to Harry Golden, Mar. 1971.

[101]Gale McGee, letter to Harry Golden, 1 Aug. 1966; Ernest Hollings, letter to Harry Golden, 3 March 1969; Ralph Yarborough, letter to Harry Golden, 9 Dec. 1964; Philip Hart, letter to Harry Golden, 16 Apr. 1969; Howard Baker, Jr., letter to Harry Golden, 24 Jan. 1978; Frank Church, letter to Harry Golden, 18 Oct. 1961; J.W. Fulbright, letter to Harry Golden, 19 Oct. 1961; Claiborne Pell letter to Harry Golden, 13 May 1962; Ernest Gruening, letter to Harry Golden, 31 Jul. 1962; Joseph Clark, letter to Harry Golden, 9 Apr. 1963; Eugene McCarthy, letter to Harry Golden, 17 Nov. 1964; Thomas Dodd, letter to Harry Golden, 25 Nov. 1964; Thomas Eagleton, letter to Harry Golden, 22 Aug. 1974; Vance Hartke, letter to Harry Golden, 31 Oct. 1974, Box 20 File 18, Harry Golden Collection Part II, U of North Carolina at Charlotte; Jacob Javits, letter to Harry Golden, 3 Jul. 1963, Box 10 File 8, Harry Golden Collection Part II, U North Carolina at Charlotte.

[102]See Appendix A for a discussion of the civil rights movement, including race riots.

[103]Abraham Ribicoff, letter to Harry Golden, 14 Oct. 1966, Box 17 File 21, Harry Golden Collection Part II, U of North Carolina at Charlotte.

[104]Ribicoff, letter to Harry Golden, 14 Oct. 1966.

[105]Harry Golden, letter to Abraham Ribicoff, 19 Oct. 1966, Box 17 File 21, Harry Golden Collection Part II, U of North Carolina at Charlotte; Abraham Ribicoff, letter to Harry Golden, 21 Oct. 1966, Box 17 File 21, Harry Golden Collection Part II, U of North Carolina at Charlotte; Harry Golden, "My Testimony Before the Senate Committee," the *Carolina Israelite* Nov./Dec. 1966: 1; Harry Golden, "The Senate Hearing," the *Carolina Israelite* Nov./Dec. 1966: 8.

[106]United States Senate, Committee on government Operations, Subcommittee on Executive Reorganization, *Federal Role in Urban Affairs* 89th Cong., 2nd sess., (Washington, D.C.: GPO, 1966) 1531.

[107]Senate, *Federal Role in Urban Affairs* 1530-1531.

[108]Senate, *Federal Role in Urban Affairs* 1539.

[109]Senate, *Federal Role in Urban Affairs* 1563.

[110]Harrison Williams, "The South's Great Victory," *Congressional Record* Senate, 88th Cong., 1st sess., (Washington, D.C.: GPO, 1963) 10589.

[111]Williams, "The South's Great Victory" 10589.

[112]Philip Hart, "Race and Immigration," *Congressional Record Senate*, 88th Cong., 2nd sess., (Washington, D.C.: GPO, 1964) 23607.

[113]Philip Hart, "The Importance of Education," *Congressional Record* Senate, 89th Cong., 1st sess., (Washington, D.C.: GPO, 1965) 2833.

[114]Hart, "The Importance of Education" 2833.

[115]Hart, "The Importance of Education" 2834.

[116]James Murray, letter to Harry Golden, 25 Mar. 1958, Box 20 File 18, Harry Golden Collection Part II, U of North Carolina at Charlotte. See Chapter 2, note #1 for information on the fire.

[117]James Murray, "Charlotte's Harry Golden: Portrait of a Pleasant Myth," *Congressional Record--Appendix* Senate (Washington, D.C.: GPO, 1958) A2697.

[118]Charles Jonas, letter to Robert Wallace, 29 April 1969, Box 20 File 17, Harry Golden Collection Part II, U of North Carolina at Charlotte; Charles Jonas, "statement" at Harry Golden Day luncheon, 19 May 1969, Harry Golden Collection, William Goldhurst Private Holdings, Gainesville.

[119]Charles Jonas, "statement" at Harry Golden day luncheon. See Chapter 2 for a discussion of the Vertical Negro Plan.

[120]Donald Fraser, letter to Harry Golden, 27 July 1964, Box 20 File 17, Harry Golden Collection Part *Israelite*, U of North Carolina at Charlotte.

[121]Barrat O'Hara, letter to Harry Golden, 11 July 1961, Box 20 File 17, Harry Golden Collection Part II, U of North Carolina at Charlotte.

[122]A.W. Joslyn, letter to Harry Golden, 8 Jan. 1965, Box 20 File 17, Harry Golden Collection Part II, U of North Carolina at Charlotte.

[123]Nick Galifianakis, letter to Harry Golden, 22 June 1972, Box 20 File 17, Harry Golden Collection Part *Israelite*, U of North Carolina at Charlotte.

[124]Seymour Halpern, letter to Harry Golden, 28 Mar. 1972; Leonard Farbstein, letter to Harry Golden, 6 Jan. 1966; Steven Derounian, letter to Harry Golden, 18 Aug. 1964; Emanuel Celler, letter to Harry Golden, 19 Aug. 1965; Herbert Zelenko, letter to Harry Golden, 13 June 1962; Edward Koch, letter to Harry Golden, 5 Feb. 1971; Elizabeth Holtzman, letter to Harry Golden, 27 Sept. 1974; James Broyhill, letter to Harry Golden, 22 Feb. 1973; Norman Martin, letter to Harry Golden, 15 Feb. 1973; Roy Taylor, letter to Harry Golden, 14 Feb. 1973; Horace Kornegay, letter to Harry Golden, 15 Aug. 1961; Robert Drinan, letter to Harry Golden, 6 May 1971; Michael Harrington, letter to Harry Golden, 9 Dec. 1975; Melvin Laird, letter to Harry Golden, 17 Aug. 1964; Roger Morton, letter to Harry Golden, 27 Aug. 1964; Clark MacGregor, letter to Harry Golden, 1 Oct. 1964; John Culver, letter to Harry Golden, 26 Nov. 1968; William Anderson, letter to Harry Golden, 15 Sept.

1971, Box 20 File 17, Harry Golden Collection Part II, U of North Carolina at Charlotte.

[125]Although Golden was praised by most of the federal legislators who were familiar with his work, on at least one occasion (in March of 1960) he found opposition in Congress to his views. According to Representative Lewis Forrester of Georgia, Golden and others mistakenly believed that civil rights legislation could cure all the ills of the country. Lewis Forrester, "Civil Rights," *Congressional Record* House (Washington, D.C.: GPO, 1960) 5211.

[126]Ogden Reid, letter to Harry Golden, 29 April 1972, Harry Golden Collection, William Goldhurst Private Holdings, Gainesville; United States House of Representatives, Committee on the Judiciary, *School Busing* 92nd Cong., 2nd sess., (Washington, D.C.: GPO, 1972) 641-644.

[127]House of Representatives, *School Busing* 641-643.

[128]Reid, letter to Harry Golden, 9 Mar. 1972.

[129]See Chapter 2 for a discussion of the Out-of-Order Plan.

[130]Charles Diggs, "How to Solve the Segregation Problem," *Congressional Record--Appendix* House (Washington, D.C.: GPO, 1957) A2832.

[131]See Chapter 2 for a discussion of the use of the Out-of-Order Plan.

[132]James Roosevelt, "The Golden Out-of-Order Plan in Operation," *Congressional Record--Appendix* House (Washington, D.C.: GPO, 1958) A6714.

[133]Roosevelt, A6714.

[134]See Chapter 2 for a discussion of the White Baby Plan.

[135]Charles Diggs, "How to Solve the Segregation Problem--The White Baby Plan," *Congressional Record--Appendix* House (Washington, D.C.: GPO, 1957) A4477-A4478.

[136]Charles Weltner, "A 20th Century Committee of Correspondence," *Congressional Record House*, 89th Cong., 2nd sess., (Washington, D.C.: GPO, 1966) 28327.

[137]Harry Golden, letter to Charles Weltner, in Charles Weltner, "A 20th Century Committee of Correspondence," *Congressional Record* House, 89th Cong., 2nd sess., (Washington, D.C.: GPO, 1966) 28328.

[138]Newton Minow, letter to Harry Golden, 10 Sept. 1962, Box 13 File 36, Harry Golden Collection Part II, U of North Carolina at Charlotte; Harry Golden, letter to Newton Minow, 17 Sept. 1962, Box 13 File 36, Harry Golden Collection Part II, U of North Carolina at Charlotte.

[139]Newton Minow, letter to Harry Golden, 30 Aug. 1961, Box 13 File 36, Harry Golden Collection Part II, U of North Carolina at Charlotte.

[140]John Buggs, letter to Harry Golden, Jan. 1974, Box 5 File 14, Harry Golden Collection Part II, U of North Carolina at Charlotte.

[141]Buggs, letter to Harry Golden, Jan. 1974.

[142]See Appendix A for a discussion of this case.

[143]Buggs, letter to Harry Golden, Jan. 1974.

[144]Mac Secrest, letter to Harry Golden, 24 Nov. 1964, Box 20 File 12, Harry Golden Collection Part II, U of North Carolina at Charlotte; See also Department of Commerce correspondence, Box 20 File 12, Harry Golden Collection Part II, U of North Carolina at Charlotte; Harold Howe, letter to Harry Golden, 12 Dec. 1968, Box 20 File 13, Harry Golden Collection Part II, U of North Carolina at Charlotte, See also Department of Health Education and Welfare correspondence, Box 20 File 13, Harry Golden Collection Part II, U of North Carolina at Charlotte; Michael Cieplinski, letter to Harry Golden, 12 Aug. 1964, Box 20 File 16, Harry Golden Collection Part II, U of North Carolina at Charlotte, See also Department of State correspondence, Box 20 File 16, Harry Golden Collection Part II, U of North Carolina at Charlotte; John Doar, letter to Harry Golden, 10 Oct. 1963, Box 20 File 15, Harry Golden Collection Part II, U of North Carolina at Charlotte, See also Department of Justice correspondence, Box 20 File 15, Harry Golden Collection Part II, U of North

Carolina at Charlotte; Holley Bell, letter to Harry Golden, 6 Dec. 1966, Box 20 File 14, Harry Golden Collection Part II, U of North Carolina at Charlotte, See also U.S. Information Agency correspondence, Box 20 File 14, Harry Golden Collection Part II, U of North Carolina at Charlotte.

[145]According to Golden, his readership also included Christian and Jewish religious leaders; government and political leaders; business and industry leaders; newspaper publishers, editors, and writers; lawyers and doctors; and many famous people. See Harry Golden, "Readership," the *Carolina Israelite* March/April 1959: 9; and Harry Golden, *Only in America* (Cleveland: World, 1958) 13.

[146]Readership of the *Carolina Israelite* ranged from 400 in 1941 to 53,000 in 1959. See Harry Golden, "25th Anniversary," the *Carolina Israelite* Nov./Dec. 1966; Harry Golden, "Net Circulation," the *Carolina Israelite* Oct. 1959: 12; Harry Golden, "Net Circulation," the *Carolina Israelite* May 1959: 9; and Harry Golden, "The Carolina Israelite's Printing," the *Carolina Israelite* Feb. 1957: 1.

[147]Edythe Rubinsohn, *The Harry Golden Followers Newsletter* May 1968; Edythe Rubinsohn, *The Harry Golden Followers Newsletter* June 1968.

[148]Belmont Abbey College, honorary degree to Harry Golden, May 1962; Johnson C. Smith University, honorary degree to Harry Golden, May 1965; Thiel College, honorary degree to Harry Golden, May 1974, Awards Series Box 159, Harry Golden Collection Part I, U of North Carolina at Charlotte; University of North Carolina at Charlotte, honorary degree to Harry Golden, May 1977, Awards Series Box 159, Harry Golden Collection Part I, U of North Carolina at Charlotte, William Goldhurst Private Holdings, Gainesville.

[149]Carver College, plaque to Harry Golden, May 1955, Awards Series Box 159, Harry Golden Collection Part I, U of North Carolina at Charlotte; Harry Golden, "Citation from Carver College," the *Carolina Israelite* June 1966: 3; University of North Carolina at Charlotte, Harry Golden Day

proclamation, & May 1969, Box 2 File 37, Harry Golden Collection Part II, University of North Carolina at Charlotte; E.K. Fretwell, Jr., letter to Harry Golden, Jr., 2 Nov. 1981, Harry Golden Collection, William Goldhurst, Private Holdings, Gainesville.

[150]U of North Carolina at Charlotte, Harry Golden Day proclamation, 7 May 1969, Box 2 File 37, Harry Golden Collection Part II, U of North Carolina at Charlotte.

[151]"Harry Golden Lectureship," *UNC-C News* Summer 1969: 3.

[152]"Five are Named to Hall of Fame," *JAFA News* April 1983: 1; Harry Golden, Jr., letter to Robin Brabham, 12 May 1983, Harry Golden Collection, William Goldhurst Private Holdings, Gainesville.

[153]"Five are Named to Hall of Fame" 2.

[154]The other founding editor of *Freedom's Journal* was Rev. Samuel Cornish; See Edwin Emery and Michael Emery, *The Press and America: An Interpretive History of the Mass Media* 5th ed. (Englewood Cliffs: Prentice-Hall, 1984) 181; National Newspaper Publishers Association, "Russwurm Award" presented to Harry Golden, 15 Mar. 1958, Awards Series Box 159, Harry Golden Collection Part I, U of North Carolina at Charlotte.

[155]Elks Grand Lodge, "Lovejoy Award" plaque to Harry Golden, 24 Aug. 1964, Awards Series Box 159, Harry Golden Collection Part I, U of North Carolina at Charlotte; Harry Golden, "The Lovejoy Award," the *Carolina Israelite* Oct. 1964: 23.

[156]Omega Psi Phi, plaque to Harry Golden, 1 May 1960, Awards Series Box 159, Harry Golden Collection Part I, U of North Carolina at Charlotte.

[157]National Association for the Advancement of Colored People, "Hall of Fame" plaque to Harry Golden, 23 May 1986, Awards Series Box 159, Harry Golden Collection Part I, U of North Carolina at Charlotte.

[158]National Association for the Advancement of Colored People, "Hall of Fame" plaque to Harry Golden, 23 May 1986, Awards Series Box 159, Harry Golden Collection Part I, U of North Carolina at Charlotte.

[159]National Association for the Advancement of Colored People, "1986 Freedom Fund Banquet" program, 23 May 1986, Awards Series Box 159, Harry Golden Collection Part I, U of North Carolina at Charlotte.

[160]National Federation of Temple Brotherhoods, "Man of the Year" plaque to Harry Golden, 15 Jan. 1959, Awards Series Box 159, Harry Golden Collection Part I, U of North Carolina at Charlotte.

[161]Agudas and Beth Israel Brotherhoods, Man of the Year" plaque to Harry Golden, 14 April 1959, Awards Series Box 159, Harry Golden Collection Part I, U of North Carolina at Charlotte.

[162]American Jewish Committee-Anti Defamation League, "Distinguished Journalism" plaque to Harry Golden, 18 June 1959, Awards Series Box 159, Harry Golden Collection Part I, U of North Carolina at Charlotte.

[163]Brith Abraham, "Grand Master Award" plaque to Harry Golden, 27 June 1960, Awards Series Box 159, Harry Golden Collection Part I, U of North Carolina at Charlotte.

[164]Brith Abraham, "Grand Master Award" plaque to Harry Golden, 27 June 1960, Awards Series Box 159, Harry Golden Collection Part I, U of North Carolina at Charlotte.

[165]State of North Carolina, "Ambassador of Goodwill" plaque to Harry Golden, 3 Dec. 1957, Awards Series Box 159, Harry Golden Collection Part I, U of North Carolina at Charlotte; Mary Semans, letter to Harry Golden, 19 July 1979, Harry Golden Collection, William Goldhurst Private Holdings, Gainesville; James A. Graham, letter to Harry Golden, 3 Dec. 1979, Box 2 File 40, Harry Golden Collection Part II, U of North Carolina at Charlotte.

[166]City Council, City of Chicago, Illinois, "A Resolution" on Harry Golden, 6 Oct. 1981, Harry Golden Collection, William Goldhurst Private Holdings, Gainesville.

[167]Public School 20 Alumni Association, certificate to Harry Golden, 19 June 1959, Awards Series Box 159, Harry Golden Collection Part I, U of North Carolina at Charlotte.

[168]Old North State Medical Society, plaque to Harry Golden, 16 June 1965, Awards Series Box 159, Harry Golden Collection Part I, U of North Carolina at Charlotte.

[169]Thomas R. Brooks, *Walls Come Tumbling Down: A History of the Civil Rights Movement, 1940-1970* (Englewood Cliffs: Prentice-Hall, 1974) 147-148; See Chapter 2 for a discussion of the Vertical Negro and Out-of-Order Plans.

[170]Robert Penn Warren, *Who Speaks for the Negro* (New York: Random House, 1965) i, 153.

[171]Bradford Daniels, *Black, White, and Gray: Twenty One Points of View on the Race Question* (New York: Libraries, 1964) vii, viii, 5-13.

[172]Taylor Branch, *Parting the Waters: America in the King Years 1954-1963* (New York: Simon and Schuster, 1988) 1006.

[173]Calder M. Pickett, *Voices of the Past: Key Documents in the History of American Journalism* (Columbus: Grid, 1977) 453.

[174]Harry Ashmore, *Hearts and Minds* (New York: McGraw Hill, 1982) 100-103; Ralph McGill, *No Place to Hide: The South and Human Rights* (Macon: Mercer U.P., 1984) 267; See Appendix B for a discussion of Harry Ashmore and Ralph McGill.

CHAPTER FOUR

SUMMARY AND CONCLUSIONS

In addition to a discussion of the historical setting in which Golden lived and worked (see Appendix A), this book addressed several broad questions dealing with Golden's motivation, method, and significance.

Golden's Motivation

Why did Harry Golden advocate civil rights for black Americans? Golden could have lived a relatively inconspicuous life. He could have devoted his post-prison life to the pursuit of personal comfort and anonymity. Likewise, he could have yielded to the southern racial relations status quo and ignored the desperate plight of southern blacks. However, Golden was compelled to participate in the struggle for black civil rights by factors such as his Jewish heritage, immigrant background, sense of morality, and sense of journalistic responsibility.

As a Jew, Golden reached the conclusion that most of his fellow Jews in the South were reluctant to take part in the civil rights movement. He believed that some Jews feared reprisals--economic and physical--from southern white gentiles, while other southern Jews had no sympathy for blacks.[1] Golden, on the other hand, utilized his Jewish heritage as a motivating factor in fighting for blacks.

Golden empathized with the suffering of blacks based on similar suffering endured by his own ancestors throughout history. He believed that the barriers of color and religion kept blacks and Jews, respectively, from full acceptance by white gentiles. He also believed that the hopes of blacks and Jews for equality and acceptance by the predominantly white gentile American society were equally intense.[2] His perception of commonality in black and Jewish suffering, hopes, and aspirations led him to believe that the struggle for black civil rights directly related to Jews. He contended that both blacks and Jews could benefit from the fight. In essence, he believed that when Jews fought for blacks, Jews fought for themselves.[3]

As an immigrant, Golden became a patriot. He, like many immigrants,[4] loved his new country with its vast opportunity and potential for individual self-fulfillment. Golden could have pursued the "American dream"[5] without concern for others. Yet, life in America proved that the dream was flawed. Golden reached the conclusion that American society was "blemished" by a "second-class citizenship"[6] imposed upon blacks. As a lover of American ideals like freedom, equality, and opportunity, Golden asserted that the condoning of the black second-class citizenship by whites was hypocrisy. Therefore, Golden believed that even though blacks were identified with the need for civil rights, the fight for civil rights was one for all Americans.[7]

As a moral human being, Golden became outraged by what he perceived as the "dehumanizing"[8] of blacks by southern whites. He considered the plight of blacks in the South desperate. Southern traditions that placed blacks in subservient roles "nagged" Golden.[9] Institutionalized racism--segregation--offended Golden because it placed him, as a white, in the capacity of an involuntary accomplice to racial inequality. Therefore, Golden wanted to do something about it. Golden wanted to make a meaningful contribution to the righting of wrong, although such a contribution provided the potential for exposing his prison past.[10]

As a socially responsible journalist, Golden believed that the American press had a duty to address serious "social ills" such as racism and segregation. He could have operated a strictly Jewish community newspaper. However, he was aware of a deliberate void in the coverage of blacks and the movement by the southern white press. Golden knew that blacks were ignored, downplayed, and portrayed in a demeaning light by the southern white press. He believed that the "story" of the movement had to be his story.[11]

Golden felt that public awareness of racial problems could foster understanding and better race relations. He saw racism as the root of unfair and unequal treatment of blacks. Therefore, he attacked various manifestations of racism, such as the denial of voting rights, substandard health care, and inadequate educational and employment opportunities for blacks.[12]

The combination of these motivating factors provided Golden with the strength of spirit to fight for what he believed was right. Thus, he undertook the fight. These motivating factors also provided him with the commitment to withstand opposition from both his fellow Jews and southern white gentiles.[13]

Golden's Method

How did Harry Golden advocate civil rights for black Americans? Based on the aforementioned factors of motivation, Golden was compelled to advocate civil rights for black Americans. Golden's motivation also related to his methods of advocacy.

Golden's journalism career began prior to his enlightenment regarding the plight of blacks in the South. Subsequently, when he became familiar with the plight of blacks and recognized the void in southern white press coverage of blacks, he was already a part of the profession that provided tremendous potential for facilitation--exposure, advocacy, amplification--of social change. As a member of the American press, Golden was in a position which provided him with the potential to rouse the conscience of the public and impel people to confront ideas concerning morality that they might have otherwise avoided. Therefore, Golden utilized journalism--the press--as his dominant outlet for civil rights advocacy.[14]

Specifically, Golden utilized personal journalism as a means of social change--civil rights--facilitation. Through personal journalism, he was able to work free of the restraints of supervision and organizational policy that routinely applied to all journalists at larger and company-operated newspapers. As a personal journalist, Golden had complete editorial control of his own newspaper. He was free to take unpopular stands and advocate causes such as civil rights for blacks. Golden's personal journalism also provided him with the freedom to utilize creative methods of advocacy, such as various forms of satiric humor.[15]

Golden used frank, satiric humor as a tool to facilitate better interracial communication, understanding, and acceptance. He wrote about the struggle for black civil rights by vividly illustrating the absurdity of racism and the ludicrous nature of segregationist traditions. Golden believed that the use of humor increased the likelihood that people would pay attention to his point of view.[16]

Just as Golden's career as a journalist had a bearing on his selection of journalism as a dominant means of civil rights advocacy, his Jewish heritage had an impact on his use of satire in journalistic advocacy of civil rights. He considered humor "a part of the Jewish culture."[17] To Golden, Jewish humor was born of a need to mitigate centuries of "despair, poverty, and terror in Europe."[18] He contended that Jewish humor was a defense against a "hostile society."[19] He also believed that "the more desperate the problem, the more humor was needed."[20] Golden in essence transferred the tradition of Jewish use of humor in desperate situations to his advocacy of civil rights for blacks.[21]

Golden's incorporation of satiric humor in his personal journalism took various forms. His Golden Plans provided seemingly ridiculous recommendations for resolving race-related problems. In addition, he used other satiric editorial forms like awards, poems, and anecdotes based on race-related themes.[22]

Golden used personal journalism as a weapon in the struggle for black civil rights. He used satiric humor as ammunition. In so doing, Golden's use of the press served to assist the black quest for civil rights.

Golden primarily used advocacy and amplification as forms of facilitation. Through advocacy, Golden supported and recommended the ideals of racial harmony--such as understanding and acceptance--and stressed the need for the attainment of civil rights for blacks. He reminded the public of American ideals--equality, justice, opportunity--

while constantly pointing out the gap between those ideals and the harsh reality of life for blacks in the South.

Golden's advocacy also complemented the work of the black press. Through targeting the *Israelite* at whites, he helped to expand such advocacy beyond the bounds of the black audience, thereby promoting sympathy and support among whites. His opinions positively influenced the civil rights thinking of a variety of whites. His advocacy not only appealed to average citizens, but to Presidents, Senators, Congressmen, Supreme Court Justices, and other governmental leaders.[23]

Although the *Israelite* was not aimed specifically at blacks, Golden's advocacy was appreciated by blacks. The black press recognized the significant complementary function Golden's journalism performed. Various black organizations also praised his efforts.[24]

Through amplification as a form of facilitation, Golden helped to magnify the importance and impact of the civil rights movement, its purpose, objectives, and activities. He helped the movement reach higher and wider levels of public awareness by amplifying the message of the movement. In the process, Golden inspired and won the respect, admiration, and appreciation of top black civil rights leaders.[25]

Golden's Significance

Did Harry Golden's journalistic work on behalf of black civil rights make a difference? A variety of people--average citizens through Presidents--were aware of Golden's advocacy. In addition, many of the people who had a direct impact on the progress and outcome of the movement--governmental and civil rights leaders--found Golden's advocacy appealing, enlightening, and inspiring. However, Golden's work takes on a greater significance in terms of overall press facilitation of the movement. His personal journalism on behalf of black civil rights also has larger implications.

Press Significance

By the late 1960s, the combined efforts of various segments of the press--black, national, print, broadcast--served to assist the modern civil rights movement. Although the press did not initiate the movement, it did expose racial injustice; advocate racial equality; and amplify the actions, objectives, and significance of the movement. Some researchers have even contended that the movement would have taken longer to achieve success--popular and governmental support, legislation--or would not have succeeded at all if not for the facilitation of the press.

Harry Golden was one of the relatively few whites who pioneered the journalistic advocacy of the modern movement in white-owned publications. He helped to lead the way in press support of the movement. Regrettably, the combination of poor health and a shift in the direction of the movement toward militancy (in the late 1960s) caused Golden to close the *Israelite* and curtail his journalistic activities. However, his journalistic support of black civil rights exemplified the dedication and zeal with which other segments of the press would eventually assist the movement. In addition, his early--1950s--advocacy also complemented the work of the black press and helped to fill a void left by the southern white press.[26]

Overall, the bravery and sacrifice of civil rights movement participants and the dedication of the press contributed to a mutually beneficial relationship between the press and the movement. The relationship provided the press with one of the most important stories of the century and the opportunity to participate in the righting of wrong. The relationship also facilitated the movement by stimulating the popular and governmental support that contributed to social change. Through the *Carolina Israelite*, Harry Golden played a significant part in the formation and perpetuation of the relationship.

Larger Implications

Despite his commitment and work on behalf of black civil rights, Golden believed that blacks were capable of fighting their own fight. However, he was compelled to help.[27] Although the civil rights movement would have taken place without Golden's help, the movement probably would not have accomplished many of its goals without the complementary participation of whites such as Golden.

Golden's advocacy was atypical of southern white involvement in the movement. Therefore, his compulsion to help and his actual advocacy take on an added dimension beyond the aforementioned motivating factors. Golden's advocacy illustrated the fact that the civil rights struggle went beyond race to encompass the issue of human equality. His desire to help illustrated a growing national intolerance with inhumanity and an awareness within American society that the unjust deprivation of the rights of any one group of people in fact diminishes the rights of all others. Harry Golden's journalistic civil rights advocacy made a difference because he had the desire to make a difference. Harry Golden had the desire to make a difference because he was involved in mankind.

Chapter Four Notes

[1]Harry Golden, *The Right Time, An Autobiography, by Harry Golden* (New York: Putnam, 1969) 238; Harry Golden, "Jew and Gentile in the New South," *Commentary* Nov. 1955: 412; Harry Golden, "Integration and the Jews," *Carolina Israelite* Mar./April 1960: 7. Many northern Jews did support and participate in the civil rights movement. See Lenwood Davis, *Black Jewish Relations in the United States, 1752-1984* (Westport: Greenwood, 1984) xi-xiii; Gus Solomon *The Jewish Role in the American Civil Rights Movement* (London: Jewish World Congress, 1967) 22; Harry Golden, "Letter to an Angry Jew," *Carolina Israelite* Sept./Oct. 1960: 17.

[2]Harry Golden, "Harry Golden," *Negro and Jew: An Encounter in America* ed. Shlomo Katz (New York: Macmillan, 1967) 64.

[3]Harry Golden, *Harry Golden on Various Matters* (New York: Anti-Defamation League of B'nai B'rith, 1966) 47.

[4]Irving Howe, *World of Our Fathers* (New York: Simon and Schuster, 1976) 34-35, 163.

[5]Harry Golden, "The American Dream," *Johns Hopkins Magazine* April 1962: 8.

[6]Golden, "The American Dream," 36-37.

[7]Harry Golden, *Ess, Ess Mein Kindt* (New York: Putnam, 1966) 212-213.

[8]Golden, *The Right Time* 239.

[9]Golden, *The Right Time* 242.

[10]Harry Golden, *For 2 Cents Plain* (Cleveland: World, 1958) 20; Golden, *The Right Time* 154-155, 210.

[11]Golden, *The Right Time* 239; Henry Lewis Suggs, *The Black Press in the South, 1865-1979* (Westport: Greenwood, 1983) 28, 142; Harry Golden, "Civil Rights for a Selfish Reason," *Carolina Israelite* April 1964: 9; Harry Golden, interview, *Sunday Morning* CBS TV 25 Oct. 1981.

[12]Golden, *For 2 Cents Plain* 251; Golden, *The Right Time* 246; Golden, "The American Dream" 8.

[13]See Chapter 2 for a discussion of opposition to Golden and the *Israelite.*

[14]To a lesser extent, Golden also utilized books (many of which were compilations of *Israelite* material), television appearances, and various speaking engagements (conventions, graduations, and Congressional hearings) to advocate civil rights for blacks.

[15]See Chapter 2, note #9, for a discussion of personal journalism.

[16]William Goldhurst, "My Father, Harry Golden," *Midstream* June/July 1969: 68, 73; William Goldhurst, personal interviews, 27 Feb. 1989, 30 Mar. 1990.

[17]Harry Golden, *The Golden Book of Jewish Humor* (New York: Putnam, 1972) 12.

[18]Harry Golden, "Jewish Wit," *Carolina Israelite* Dec. 1965: 5.

[19]Golden, "Jewish Wit" 5.

[20]Golden, *The Golden Book of Jewish Humor* 12.

[21]William Goldhurst, personal interview, 30 Mar. 1990; Golden, *The Golden Book of Jewish Humor* 11.

[22]See Chapter 2 for discussions of the Golden Plans and anecdotes and other forms of satire used by Golden.

[23]Golden, *The Right Time* 252; See Chapter 3 for a discussion of Golden's appeal.

[24]For example, the National Newspaper Publishers Association, an organization of the leaders of most black

newspapers published in America, honored Golden for his journalistic advocacy. In addition, other black organizations such as the Elks Grand Lodge and the Omega Psi Phi fraternity honored Golden for his advocacy on behalf of blacks. See Chapter 3 for a discussion of Golden's institutional honors.

[25]See Chapter 3 for a discussion of Golden and the civil rights community.

[26]Other white journalistic advocates included people like Ralph McGill, Harry Ashmore, P.D. East, and Hodding Carter. See Appendix B for a discussion of such journalists. See Chapter 2 for a discussion of the closing of the *Israelite*.

[27]Golden *Sunday Morning* CBS.

Appendix A

An Overview of the Quest for Black Civil Rights in America

The civil rights advocacy of Harry Golden was indicative of his concern about the plight of black Americans. He was outraged by racism, segregation, and the resulting cruelty inflicted by whites and endured by blacks.[1] The arena of civil rights was Golden's battlefield. The press--personal journalism--was his weapon. His humor, outspokenness, and dedication were his ammunition. In essence, the people and events of the civil rights movement, as well as Golden's concern for blacks as fellow human beings, served to influence and mold his writing.

Based on the relevant historical literature, this overview provides an examination of the arena of civil rights for readers who a) were born after the movement or b) are not familiar with the movement. First, this appendix concentrates on the rights, freedoms, disenfranchisement, and subjugation of blacks prior to the modern civil rights movement. Next, the factors which collectively led to the movement and its implementation are explored. Finally, an overview of the major events, leaders, organizations, and accomplishments of the movement is presented.

Prelude to a Modern Movement

After gaining freedom from slavery through Presidential proclamation and national civil war,[2] blacks attempted to participate in American society as free individuals. Blacks served on juries, participated in state militias, voted,[3] and served in the federal and state governments.[4] However, as the former Confederate states and citizens of the South rejoined the Union and sought the political and economic power lost through the war, blacks were systematically denied democratic and civil rights as well as equality with whites. Instead of being assimilated into American society, blacks, as during slavery, were once again subjugated by whites.[5]

During Reconstruction, blacks had begun to achieve political strength. Between 1867 and 1868, qualified black voters outnumbered qualified white voters 703,400 to 660,000 in the former Confederate states.[6] Although blacks only constituted a minority in state and federal governmental offices,[7] between 1869 and 1876 sixteen blacks served in the United States Congress,[8] On the state level, blacks served in the legislatures of Alabama, Florida, Louisiana, Mississippi, North Carolina and South Carolina.[9] In addition, blacks held a variety of other state offices including Lieutenant Governor, Secretary of State, State Treasurer, Supreme Court Justice, and Superintendent of Education.[10]

Between the late 1860s and mid-1870s, southerners--former Confederates--attempted to regain their United States citizenship and property,[11] and southern states rejoined the union.[12] The former Confederate states held conventions, wrote new constitutions, and established new--reconstructionist--governments.[13] However, usually upon the readmission of a state, conservatives like the southern Democratic Party and the Conservative Union Party began opposing the new state's administration as well as black involvement in government.[14] As new state governments were established, the conservatives routinely predicted the governments' failure.[15]

Using the presumed inferiority and ineptness of blacks for participation in government as a smoke screen for their attempt to regain pre-Civil War political and economic power over blacks, white racist forces, such as the Conservative Democrats and the Ku Klux Klan, pursued the systematic disenfranchisement of blacks. The denial of black suffrage was implemented through manipulation of the voting process and enforced through economic intimidation and violence. In addition, the tenets of race separation and racial inequality flourished.[16]

In order to regain political power over blacks, southern whites manipulated the voting process in various ways. For example, white-only primaries, through which the Democratic party confined voting to white voters, were utilized.[17] Gerrymandering, through which voting districts were drawn or re-drawn, was also implemented in order to minimize the potential of black voting strength.[18] In addition, an eight-ballot-box system was developed through which eight instead of one ballot boxes were used in an attempt to confuse illiterate black voters. Through this system, states such as Florida used different boxes for the various posts being contested and ballots put in the wrong boxes were not counted.[19]

Potential black voters also faced other obstacles. For example, polling places were moved at the last minute without the notification of blacks.[20] Through literacy testing, the prospective black voters had to demonstrate familiarity with their state constitution to white registration officials who were empowered to pass or fail applicants--blacks usually failed.[21] In addition, a grandfather clause was utilized through which the right to vote was only extended to individuals whose grandfathers possessed the right to vote on January 1, 1867-- predominantly whites.[22]

In an attempt to regain economic power over blacks, some southern states enacted Black Codes in an attempt to restore control and regulation of the black labor force.[23] Historian Peter Camejo contended that such codes forced blacks into "a labor caste, somewhere between chattel slaves and free but propertyless laborers."[24] In essence, blacks were placed in a legal form of second-class citizenship.[25] The black codes gave white landowners many of the benefits of slavery. For example, under the Mississippi code, which was considered severe,[26] blacks who were younger than eighteen years of age and who were orphans or whose parents could not support them were placed in the service of and under control of whites--usually their former owner. The former owner, who could administer corporal punishment, was allowed to hold females until they reached the age of eighteen and hold males until they reached the age of twenty-one.[27] In addition, all blacks who were unemployed, homeless, or found guilty of adultery, drunkenness, or theft could be placed in the charge of their former master.[28]

White southerners used various forms of intimidation to strengthen their post-Reconstruction political and economic power over blacks. Intimidation ranged from threats of being fired by white employers to threats of denial of medical care by white doctors, and included threats of violence against black voters.[29] By far the most severe form of intimidation was the actual use of violence against blacks and whites who were sympathetic to blacks. Whippings, mutilations, burning alive, lynching, drowning, and what historian John Hope Franklin contended was "any effective means of violence conceivable"[30] awaited blacks who were insolent or who dared to vote. A similar fate awaited white supporters.[31] Camejo reported that, between 1867 and 1871 approximately 20,000 blacks and white supporters were murdered in the southern United States.[32] As black disenfranchisement--enforced by violence--flourished, blacks stopped voting in large numbers. Blacks were also ousted from state and federal governmental offices.[33] Camejo also contended that by the early twentieth century, "only two percent of the potential black electorate voted in twelve southern states."[34]

Rationale for a Modern Movement

For generations, black Americans experienced frustration and discontent over racial inequality stemming from slavery, and black disenfranchisement stemming from counter-Reconstruction. Opposition to such inequality and disenfranchisement has been present throughout the history of the United States. It has taken forms such as slave revolts, the abolitionist movement, the Underground Railroad, and the return to Africa movement.[35] Despite early opposition, black Americans of the mid-twentieth century inherited a legacy of life at the bottom of the socioeconomic ladder.[36] In 1963, this legacy prompted the United States Commission on Civil Rights[37] to conclude after a six-year investigation that "the civil rights of Negro citizens continue to be widely discarded,"[38] and also that "the descendants of freed slaves still suffer from customs, traditions, and prejudices that should have died with the institution in which they flourished."[39]

Economically, during the 1950s and 1960s many more black than white Americans lived in poverty.[40] In addition, between 1950 and 1963 the average annual income of blacks ranged from 52% to 54% of the average annual income of whites.[41] Similarly, between 1964 and 1968 the average annual income of blacks was only 55.4% of that for whites.[42] Also, during the 1950s and 1960s black unemployment ranged from 7% to 11% compared to 3% to 5% for whites.[43] Those blacks who were employed tended to be concentrated in the lower-paying menial jobs. For example, 75% of the black men in the American labor force during this time worked in unskilled jobs, such as janitors and porters. In addition, 50% of black women in the labor force worked as domestics, such as maids and cooks.[44] According to the Civil Rights Commission, "the economic plight of the Negro has its roots in segregation and discrimination,"[45] which resulted in inadequate education, inferior job training, and discrimination by private employers in the training and hiring of blacks.[46]

Politically, the early and mid-twentieth century saw the continuation of the exclusion of blacks from the political process through the use of poll taxes, voter registration testing, violence, and other forms of intimidation.[47] In 1963, the Civil Rights Commission concluded that the right to vote was not only denied to blacks for "almost 100 years," but "the right to vote is still denied" to blacks.[48] The Commission also added that in some areas of the South "virtually all the voting-age whites have been registered regardless of qualifications, while Negroes have been systematically rejected."[49]

The economic and political plight of black Americans in the early to mid-twentieth century along with the social oppression of blacks--primarily through segregation--also added to mounting black frustrations. Social oppression as a key factor in the education, housing, health care and military service of blacks enhanced the need and desire for some sort of relief--namely, a modern movement.[50] In terms of education, blacks of this period had to endure poorly equipped, segregated schools which were usually housed in sub-standard buildings. Journalist Harry Ashmore argued that the general discrimination against blacks in education stemmed from the inattentiveness of southern school officials, who were usually white.[51] He asserted that such southern school officials reflected the attitude of the majority of southern whites who believed that blacks needed no more than a basic grade school education in order to assume their proper place in society as laborers and domestics.[52] Consequently, black students were provided with inferior equipment and facilities and less funding for education than white students. For example, in the South between 1940 and 1952 less money was spent per student and on facilities for black students than for whites. In addition, black teachers were paid lower salaries than white teachers, and black schools were provided with smaller libraries, in terms of space and holdings, than white schools.[53] On the matter of segregated schools, the Civil Rights Commission found that despite the unconstitutionality of segregated schools, as determined by the 1954 Supreme Court ruling in *Brown v. Board of Education*,[54] most southern school boards during the mid-1950s through the early 1960s were determined to "evade or avoid desegregation."[55] The Commission considered segregated schools a hindrance to the preparation of "youth to function in a multiracial society as participating citizens."[56]

In the matters of housing and health care, the Commission reported that during the 1950s and early 1960s the national welfare and security required the realization of a "decent home or suitable living environment" for all Americans.[57] However, the Commission concluded that blacks were not able to purchase decent shelter freely because of high prices and the hesitancy of whites to sell to blacks.[58] In addition, the Commission pointed out that black patients and medical professionals were denied access to or were segregated in many medical care facilities. They concluded that such practices adversely affected national health standards as well as the training of black medical professionals.[59]

On the topic of military service, there were relatively few blacks in the armed forces, especially as officers and supervisory personnel, during the early to mid-twentieth century.[60] In addition, blacks were excluded from service in the Marine Corps and the Air Force and were usually relegated to domestic, unskilled and menial duties in the Army and Navy.[61] After World War I and World War II, discontent among black military personnel, concerning their lack of opportunity in the armed forces, grew as they also pondered the irony of their participation in wars abroad while they faced racism and segregation at home. Blacks returning home from the World Wars became determined to work for equality and opportunity at home and in the military.[62] In general, blacks sought desegregation and the same military training, opportunity, and advancement as whites.[63] Likewise, many southern whites were equally determined to keep blacks in their place as second-class citizens. Consequently, many blacks who returned home from military service after the wars came home to race riots and intense discrimination.[64] Historian Thomas Brooks revealed that some southern cities invested in "anti-riot weaponry in fear of armed insurrection by organized returning Negro veterans."[65]

The combination of economic and political repression and domination of blacks--enforced by violence and other forms of intimidation--along with social oppression--through discrimination and segregation as a factor in the education, housing, health care, and military service of blacks--served as a constant and mounting source of frustration and discontent for blacks. That frustration was eventually refocused into resistance to repression and oppression. Likewise, the resistance served as the foundation upon which the motivation and sacrifice of many people, black and white, would lead to a mass movement as black Americans sought a better life and the true enfranchisement which was alluded to during Reconstruction and then taken away. The modern civil rights movement would successfully evolve during the early 1950s and 1960s.

Overview of the Modern Movement

During the 1950s and 1960s, blacks and sympathetic whites worked to secure the long-denied liberty and full rights of American citizenship for blacks--civil rights. starting with the courts, in order to gain legal support and set precedent, the modern civil rights movement quickly branched out to include mass nonviolent civil disobedience through boycotts, marches, sit-ins, and other forms of demonstration. Such tactics were used in order to illustrate to the country and the world the lack of and need for civil rights. They were also used to disrupt the normal functioning of segregated institutions.[66]

Organizations

The black church served as the initial institutional center of the modern movement, according to civil rights researcher Aldon Morris. He contended that the black church provided the movement with "the leadership of clergymen skilled in the art of managing people and resources, a financial base, and meeting places."[67] This is exemplified by the fact that both Dr. Martin Luther King, Jr., the acknowledged leader of the movement,[68] and Dr. Ralph David Abernathy, King's second in command and successor,[69] were both ministers and indeed used their churches as bases of operations during the initial stages of the movement.[70] Black churches also provided blacks with an escape from the harsh reality associated with oppression by whites. Morris maintained that black churches were institutions free from the control of whites, and inside their walls blacks were "temporarily free to forget oppression."[71]

In addition to the black church, numerous other organizations, primarily civil rights organizations, influenced the momentum, direction, and impact of the modern civil rights movement. Several civil rights organizations were highly influential.

NAACP. The National Association for the Advancement of Colored People was founded in 1909 by a group of blacks and whites who were opposed to racism. The principal tactics of the organization were educational persuasion, based on the idea that whites would treat blacks as equals once whites overcame their ignorance of blacks;

and legal action, designed to attack segregation and racial inequality via the court system.[72] *Brown v. Board of Education* and other early legal victories of the civil rights movement were planned and fought by NAACP attorneys.[73]

CORE. The Congress of Racial Equality was founded in 1942 by a group of blacks and whites in order to address civil rights problems. The organization initially used and proposed the use of tactics such as sit-ins, hunger strikes, freedom rides, and mass marches as a means of civil rights demonstration.[74]

SCLC. The Southern Christian Leadership Conference was founded in 1957 by a group of black southern ministers as a formal organization of religious leaders to fight for civil rights. Under the leadership of King, the group's first President, and Abernathy, King's Vice President, the SCLC coordinated some of the earliest and most successful campaigns of the movement, such as Montgomery and Birmingham.[75] Morris asserted that the SCLC developed into the "organizational center of the movement" and functioned as an arm of the mass black church.[76]

SNCC. The Student Nonviolent Coordinating Committee was founded in 1960 by black college students who wanted an organized, but youthful, outlet for participation in the fight for civil rights. The initial tactic of the organization was the utilization of sit-ins as a form of protest against segregated public facilities. Later, other forms of protest, such as marches, were advocated by the organization.[77]

Events

The formation and momentum of the modern civil rights movement was directly influenced by a highly significant legal battle and victory that was led by the NAACP. With the Supreme Court's 1954 decision in *Brown v. Board of Education*, the doctrine of separate-but-equal, previously the foundation of legalized segregation, was ruled inherently unequal and unconstitutional in the field of public education.[78] The Brown decision established a legal precedent upon which the movement would not only test the implementation of integration in schools, but throughout American society.

The case, which consolidated four other cases,[79] grew out of the frustrations of black parents who were forced to send their children to segregated schools that were usually housed inadequate facilities, and in some states were located farther away from the black community that white schools. The NAACP attorneys who handled the case(s) argued that segregated schools imposed social and psychological handicaps upon black children by inflicting unrealistic racial isolation upon them. The attorneys asserted that black children would grow up in a country where whites composed a large majority of the population. In addition, the attorneys maintained that segregated schools retarded the educational and mental development of black children.[80] *Brown v. Board of Education* overturned an 1896 Supreme Court decision in *Plessy v. Ferguson* through which the Court had given legal validity to segregation. The separate-but-equal doctrine brought about by the *Plessy* case deemed segregation constitutional as long as blacks were provided with accommodations equal to those of whites.[81]

In 1955, the Little Rock, Arkansas school board began making plans for school integration in keeping with the mandate of *Brown v. Board of Education.* After much modification, the school board adopted a plan which would integrate one white high school with a limited number of black students within a three-year period.[82] Shortly thereafter, white opposition, supported by Arkansas Governor Orval Faubus, threatened to forestall implementation of the plan.[83] Consequently, a federal court order secured by the NAACP admonished the school board to implement the plan. The board next screened black students for potential enrollment. Eventually, nine students, "The Little Rock Nine," were selected.[84] However, prior to the actual enrollment of the black students, Governor Faubus, who was against school integration, ordered the Arkansas National Guard to surround central high school.[85] As a result, when the nine black students attempted to attend school on September 4, 1957, National Guardsmen prevented them from entering.[86]

By September 14, 1957, President Dwight Eisenhower informed Governor Faubus that Supreme Court orders had to be obeyed. Eisenhower also noted that the use of the National Guard should have been as protection for the black students rather than a hindrance to their enrollment.[87] Subsequently, Faubus recalled the National Guard. Later, when mobs of segregationists surrounded the school to prevent the attendance of the black students, the mayor of Little Rock requested and received the assistance of federal military troops.[88]

With United States Army troops surrounding the school, the Little Rock Nine finally attended class at Central High School. Army bodyguards escorted each of the black students to and from school and classes each day for several weeks, until order prevailed. The underlying theme of the Little Rock crisis--the conflict between state and federal government over the protection of civil rights--would recur in the struggle for civil rights.[89]

In 1953, blacks in Baton Rouge, Louisiana boycotted their local bus system in order to protest segregated seating. The week-long boycott did not bring an end to local segregated seating on buses.[90] However, in 1955, the first major and successful mass action of the modern civil rights movement occurred when blacks in Montgomery, Alabama successfully conducted a thirteen-month boycott of their local bus company. The boycott resulted in integrated seating on buses. As was the case throughout the South, blacks in Montgomery were required to ride in the back of local buses. Blacks also gave up their seats to whites as larger numbers of whites filled the front section and moved toward the rear. When a black woman, Mrs. Rosa Parks, was arrested for refusing to surrender her bus seat to a white passenger, the black community in Montgomery quickly mobilized, not only to support Mrs. Parks, but also to protest the unfairness and inequality of segregation. Under the leadership of King and Abernathy, and despite violence and intimidation by whites, blacks walked, car pooled, and sought legal remedy, until success--an integrated bus line--was won.[91] With the coming of the 1960s, the momentum of the new movement spread and was intensified by the support and participation of black, and later white, college students. A major tactic employed by college students was the use of sit-ins as a protest against segregated public facilities. The first such sit-in of the movement occurred during February of 1960 in Greensboro, North Carolina. At that time, four black students[92] from North Carolina Agricultural and Technical State University visited the local F.W. Woolworth department store where they sat down at the store's white-only lunch counter and attempted to place orders.[93] Although the students were refused service, word of their action spread across the South and stimulated action by other college students not only at stores, but at libraries, hotels, and beaches as well.[94]

The 1960s also witnessed the reintroduction of a protest tactic originally used by CORE. In 1947, an interracial group of CORE members attempted to ride public bus lines throughout the upper South in an attempt to confront and resist segregated seating of interstate bus passengers. The ride came to an end when the CORE members were arrested in North Carolina for violating segregation laws.[95] However, the ride later aided the modern movement by serving as a model for a new series of rides--the freedom rides--in 1961.

The 1961 freedom rides planned by CORE were designed to once again confront segregation in interstate transportation. The plan called for two interracial bus loads of CORE members to leave Washington, D.C. and travel throughout the South. During the rides, white members were to sit in the back of the buses and black members were to sit in the front. In addition, at each stop blacks would attempt to use white-only facilities--waiting rooms, rest rooms, lunch counters, and water fountains.[96] As in 1947, the 1961 riders ran into difficulty. One bus was burned by a white mob in Anniston, Alabama, while the riders of the second bus were beaten by white mobs in Birmingham and Montgomery, Alabama. Finally, under Alabama National Guard Protection, the freedom riders travelled from Montgomery to Jackson, Mississippi, only to be tried and imprisoned on their arrival. Despite the brutality inflicted upon the freedom riders, more than 300 additional riders followed in the footsteps of the initial riders throughout the summer of 1961.[97]

In April of 1963, veteran civil rights workers and the SCLC once again took the center stage for one of the most violent episodes of the movement. After the city of Birmingham, Alabama closed its municipal parks, playgrounds, swimming pools, and golf courses rather than comply with a court order to integrate them, the city was targeted by King and the SCLC for protest action.[98] The SCLC Project "C" for confrontation set out to demonstrate against segregated businesses and lunch counters in addition to seeking the reopening of the closed public recreational facilities.[99] Hundreds of arrests resulted from the demonstrations including those of King and Abernathy.[100] Upon the release of King and Abernathy from jail, they launched a "children's Crusade," which called for black school children to conduct marches in downtown Birmingham. King, Abernathy, and the SCLC believed school children could not be intimidated economically, as could their parents, and also that there was less of a chance for police brutality against children as compared to adults. According to Abernathy, "We were certain that even the most mean spirited cop would refrain from clubbing a very small child."[101] However, Birmingham Public Safety Commissioner Eugene "Bull" Connor ordered the use of high-pressure fire hoses and police dogs against the young demonstrators after attempts to jail large numbers[102] of marchers did not quell the protest. As outraged black adults joined the demonstrations, the toll of arrests went to over two thousand people.[103]

With racial tensions continuing to mount and national and international attention focused on the city, white businessmen and city officials decided, within five weeks of the start of Project "C," to work out a desegregation plan with the SCLC. The plan provided for the integration of facilities--lunch counters, rest rooms, fitting rooms, water fountains--and the hiring of black sales personnel.[104] Shortly after the settlement was reached, National Guard and U.S. Army troops were dispatched to Birmingham by President John F. Kennedy, following President Eisenhower's example in Little Rock, to quiet racial violence related to the bombing of several black homes and businesses.[105] Kennedy did not want the agreement between the SCLC and the white businessmen to be ruined by violent racism.[106]

Fresh from and in part prompted by the violence of Birmingham, as well as the overall plight of black Americans, the stage was set for the movement's largest single outpouring of popular support. That support was demonstrated in August of 1963 when 250,000 people, black and white, from all over the country converged on Washington, D.C. to attend a mass rally designed to protest racism, segregation, and racial inequality. The March on Washington was also designed to show support for a civil rights act which would provide for the fair treatment, equal opportunity, and equal access to public facilities for blacks.[107]

An earlier attempt at a march on Washington, planned by CORE in 1941, was not implemented. However, the CORE idea was successfully carried out during the 1963 march as the mass audience was presented with speeches, prayers, and music that stressed to the country and its leaders the need for equality and civil rights.[108] The day was highlighted by Martin Luther King's "I Have a Dream" speech in which King projected an America full of opportunity and free of hatred, racism, and injustice.[109] By July 2, 1964, President Lyndon B. Johnson signed the Civil Rights Act of 1964, which outlawed segregation in public accommodations. The year 1964 ended triumphantly for the movement with the December awarding of the Nobel Peace Prize to its leader. King was awarded the prize for his advocacy and use of nonviolent protest as a means of securing civil rights for blacks.[110] The movement next focused on the need for specific legislation designed to provide for the registration and protection of black voters. In 1963, blacks made up half of the voting population in Selma, Alabama. However, only one percent of voting age blacks were registered to vote. Selma's white voting officials made it difficult for blacks to register. Blacks were intimidated and the operation of the voter registration office was limited to two days per month.[111] Based on such conditions, SNCC members began an attempt to help blacks in Selma register to vote. By 1964, the SCLC was also drawn to Selma and targeted the city for demonstrations in the form of marches to the local court house on the days during which attempts at registration were allowed.[112]

At this juncture, King and the SCLC sought to illustrate to the nation the intimidation and violence encountered by blacks when attempting to register to vote. In so doing, they also sought to put pressure on the federal government for voting rights legislation that provided for federal voting registrars.[113] According to Abernathy, "we wanted a voting bill and we knew that we would never get one unless the American people saw what was going on in places like Selma."[114]

With the initiation of the SCLC's 1965 Selma demonstrations, protesters were soon brutalized by local and state law enforcement officers. On one such occasion, a protester, Jimmie Lee Jackson, was shot by an Alabama state trooper. Jackson died within a week.[115] As a result of Jackson's death, the SCLC decided to broaden the Selma protest strategy by staging a mass march--the "Alabama Freedom March"--to Montgomery and presented Alabama Governor George Wallace, who opposed the march, with a petition demanding civil rights in Alabama.[116] When six hundred people attempted to march on Sunday, March 7, 1965, they were met by numerous state troopers who use tear gas and billy clubs, while atop charging horses, to disperse the marchers. So many marchers were charged and beaten that the day of the march was dubbed "Bloody Sunday."[117]

Three days later, after word of Bloody Sunday shocked the nation, over 1,500 more potential marchers gathered in Selma to stage a second attempt. However, the second march also proved unsuccessful when King, who was leading the march, was confronted by state troopers and consequently led the marchers back to their starting point. Later, the SCLC received court approval for a third march attempt. At that time, President Johnson ordered the use of U.S. Army troops
--as did Presidents Kennedy in Birmingham and Eisenhower in Little Rock--as well as FBI agents, United States Marshals, and federalized Alabama National Guard units to protect the marchers. The number of marchers eventually swelled to 25,000 before the march reached Montgomery.

Upon their arrival in Montgomery, King and other civil rights movement leaders addressed a large crowd of supporters from the steps of the state capitol. Simultaneously, SCLC members unsuccessfully attempted to deliver the petitions to Governor Wallace.[118] By August 6, 1965, President Johnson signed a voting rights bill after earlier condemning what happened in Selma as an "American Tragedy"[119] and echoing, by way of a nationally televised address, the slogan of the movement, "We Shall Overcome."[120]

Along with the successful bid for a voting rights act, the mid- and late 1960s also witnessed the doctrine of nonviolent protest--which had been advocated by King, other movement leaders, and major civil rights organizations--come under attack and eventually decline. During this time, newer, younger, and more militant black leaders--Stokely Carmichael, H. Rap Brown, Huey Newton, and Eldridge Clever--began to advocate violent resistance to racism. Consequently, redress of racial inequality moved beyond court battles, marches, sit-ins, and other forms of peaceful protest, and toward militancy. With the 1965 race riots in Watts (Los Angeles, California) and Harlem (New York, New York) came a volatile combination of black frustrations and militancy that served to alienate some sympathetic whites and moderate blacks. In the process, militancy had a negative effect on the course, support, and intensity of the movement as a mass action.[121]

Martyrs

From slavery through the modern civil rights movement, countless numbers of blacks and whites were killed while attempting to secure freedom and equality for blacks. The civil rights movement incurred many casualties[122] including, but not limited to, several well-publicized murders. For example, Medgar Evers, a NAACP Mississippi field representative, was shot to death in 1963.[123] Similarly, SNCC student voter registration volunteers Andrew Goodman, Michael Schwerner,--both white--and James Chaney were beaten and shot to death in 1964 while working in Mississippi.[124] In addition, Jimmy Lee Jackson, a civil rights demonstrator was shot--and later died--by an Alabama state trooper while protesting in 1965.[125] James Reeb, a white minister, was beaten--and subsequently died--in 1965, by a mob while in Alabama to march with the SCLC.[126] Viola Liuzzo, a white SCLC volunteer, was shot and killed while driving SCLC freedom marchers in 1965.[127]

One of the most devastating murders, in terms of the direction of the movement, occurred in March of 1968. While in Memphis, Tennessee to support a garbage workers' strike and coordinate SCLC strategy, King was shot and killed.[128] His death brought an end to the strong central leadership of the modern movement as well as an end to an era of mass, nonviolent, highly organized protests as a means of striving for civil rights.[129]

The active life of the modern, nonviolent, civil rights movement, as well as the deaths of some of its workers and its leader were not in vain. During the course of the movement, from 1954 to 1968, many victories were won, including: the national exposure and condemnation of violent racism, the overturning of legalized segregation, the enactment of substantial federal legislation pertaining to civil rights, and the validation of nonviolent movement methods through the awarding of the Nobel Peace Prize to its leader, King.[130] In essence, the movement provided an outlet for the venting of frustrations stemming from disenfranchisement, racism, and segregation, and helped blacks realize some of the hope and dreams that were first alluded to during Reconstruction. In addition, the civil rights movement provided the press, as a whole, and specific journalistic civil rights advocates--such as Golden--with a wealth of news on which to report or comment.

Appendix A Notes

[1]Harry Golden, *The Right Time: An Autobiography, by Harry Golden* (New York: Putnam, 1969) 237, 239, 242.

[2]Avery Craven, *Reconstruction: The Ending of the Civil War* (New York: Holt, Rinehart, and Winston, 1969) 1-14.

[3]According to historian W.E.B. Dubois, some free blacks who owned land and property had the right to vote at earlier periods in American history. However, in most cases such black suffrage was taken away by state governments. Dubois noted that, prior to Reconstruction, black suffrage was taken away in the following states at the following times: South Carolina, 1716; Virginia, 1722; North Carolina, 1734; Georgia, 1761; Delaware, 1790s; Maryland, 1790s; Tennessee, 1796; Kentucky, 1799; Ohio, 1803; New Jersey, 1807; Louisiana, 1812; Connecticut, 1814; Indiana, 1816; Mississippi, 1817; Illinois, 1818; Alabama, 1819; New York, 1821; Missouri, 1821; Arkansas, 1836; Michigan, 1837; Pennsylvania, 1838; Texas, 1845; Florida, 1845; Iowa, 1846; Wisconsin, 1848; Minnesota, 1858; and Kansas, 1861. See Dubois *Black Reconstruction in America* (New York: Russell and Russell, 1935) 6-8.

[4]Peter Camejo, *Racism, Revolution, and Reaction, 1861-1877* (New York: Monad, 1976) 241; Thomas Brooks, *Walls Come Tumbling Down: A History of the Civil Rights Movement, 1940-1970* (Englewood Cliffs: Prentice-Hall, 1974) 14.

[5]Camejo 246.

[6]John Hope Franklin, *Reconstruction After the Civil War* (Chicago: University of Chicago Press, 1961) 80.

[7]LaWanda Cox, and John Cox, eds. *Reconstruction the Negro, and the New South* (Columbia: University of South Carolina Press, 1973) xxiii.

[8]Dubois 627; Franklin, 135; According to Dubois and Franklin, sixteen blacks served in the Federal Congress during this time, including: Hiram R. Revels, a Senator from

Mississippi, 1870-1871; Blanche K. Bruce, a Senator from Mississippi, 1875-1881; Jefferson P. Long, a Congressman from Georgia, 1869-1870; Joseph H. Rainey, a Congressman from South Carolina, 1871-1879; Robert C. DeLarge, a Congressman from South Carolina, 1871-1873; Robert B. Elliott, a Congressman from South Carolina, 1871-1875; Benjamin S. Turner, a Congressman from Alabama, 1871-1873; Josiah T. Walls, a Congressman from Florida, 1873-1877; Alonzo J. Ransier, a Congressman from South Carolina, 1871-1873; James T. Rapier, a Congressman from Alabama, 1873-1875; Richard H. Cain, a Congressman from South Carolina, 1873-1875, 1877-1879; John R. Lynch, a Congressman from Mississippi, 1873-1877, 1881-1883; Charles E. Nash, a Congressman from Louisiana, 1875-1877; John A. Hyman, a Congressman from North Carolina, 1875-1877; Jere Haralson, a Congressman from Alabama, 1875-1877; and Robert Smalls, a Congressman from South Carolina, 1875-1879, 1881-1887.

[9]Franklin 132-134.

[10]Franklin 133-135.

[11]Craven 111.

[12]Franklin 80.

[13]Franklin 120.

[14]Franklin 130.

[15]Franklin 129.

[16]Camejo 151; Dubois 694.

[17]Dubois 694.

[18]Camejo 197.

[19]Camejo 197.

[20]Camejo 197.

[21]Camejo 198.

[22]Dubois 694; Camejo 198.

[23]Craven 119.

[24]Camejo 145.

[25]Cox xiii.

[26]Cox xiv.

[27]Craven 120-121.

[28]Craven 120-121.

[29]Camejo 153.

[30]Franklin 155.

[31]Franklin 157, 160; Camejo 145, 187.

[32]Camejo 146.

[33]Camejo 166; Franklin 130-131, 172.

[34]Camejo 199.

[35]Morris x; Brooks 8; For example, according to Lauren Kessler, Marcus Garvey preached black nationalism and the idea of returning to Africa. Garvey maintained that only by returning to their ancestral home could blacks ever achieve equality and live in social harmony, see Kessler 42.

[36]Carolyn Martindale, *The White Press and Black America* (New York: Greenwood, 1986) 4.

[37]The Civil Rights Commission was established by Congress to investigate the denial of civil rights to U.S. citizens and suggest appropriate action to Congress.

[38]United States, Commission on Civil Rights, *Civil Rights '63* (Washington, D.C., U.S. Government Printing Office, 1963) 1.

[39]U.S. Commission 2.

[40]Martindale 5.

[41]For example, according to Juan Williams, in 1963 the national average annual income was $6,500 while only $3,500 for blacks; See Williams *Eyes on the Prize* (New York: Penguin, 1988) 197; In addition, Martindale reported that black average annual income had only risen to 61% of white income by 1969, see Martindale 5.

[42]Harrell Rodgers, Jr. "Civil Rights and the Myth of Popular Sovereignty,: *Journal of Black Studies* 12.1 (1981): 56-57.

[43]Williams 197; Brooks 87; Aldon Morris, *The Origins of the Civil Rights Movement: Black Communities Organizing for Change* (New York: Macmillan, 1984) 1; Martindale 5.

[44]Morris 1; U.S. Commission 73.

[45]U.S. Commission 91.

[46]U.S. Commission 90.

[47]Morris 2; U.S. Commission 22-23.

[48]U.S. Commission 13.

[49]U.S. Commission 22.

[50]U.S. Commission 53, 95, 129, 171.

[51]Harry Ashmore, *The Negro and the Schools* (Chapel Hill: University of North Carolina Press, 1954) 125.

[52]Ashmore 130.

[53]Ashmore 62-63.

[54]*Oliver Brown v. Board of Education of Topeka, Kansas*, 74 S.Ct. 686 and 347 U.S. 483, 1954.

[55]U.S. Commission 68.

[56]U.S. Commission 68.

[57]U.S. Commission 96.

[58]U.S. Commission 95.

[59]U.S. Commission 129.

[60]According to Thomas Brooks, by 1940 there were 5,000 blacks in the 269,023-man Army and 4,000 blacks in the 160,997-man Navy; See Brooks 9.

[61]Brooks 9; U.S. Commission 171, 214.

[62]Brooks 52, 69.

[63]Brooks 10.

[64]Lauren Kessler, *The Dissident Press* (Beverly Hills: Sage, 1984) 42.

[65]Brooks 55.

[66]Brooks 50-51; Morris xi.

[67]Morris 4.

[68]Williams 289.

[69]Williams 289; Ralph David Abernathy, *And the Walls Came Tumbling Down* (New York: Harper and Row, 1989) xii.

[70]Abernathy 136-188.

[71]Morris 4.

[72]Brooks 16, 19; Morris 12-14.

[73]Williams 3-35.

[74]Williams 125, 127; Brooks 50-51.

[75]Williams 89; Abernathy 148, 186.

[76]Morris xiii.

[77]Williams 137; Morris xiii.

[78]*Brown v. Board* 74 S.Ct. 686; Brooks 94; Williams 3-35.

[79]The other cases were: *Briggs v. Elliot* from South Carolina, 342 U.S. 350, 72 S.Ct. 327; *Davis v. County* School Board from Virginia, 103 Fed. Supp. 337; *Belton v. Gebhart* from Delaware, 344 U.S. 891; and *Bolling v. Sharpe* from Washington, D.C., 347 U.S. 497, 74 S.Ct. 693; See *Brown v. Board* 74 S.Ct. 686; Williams 27, 31; Brooks 93.

[80]Brooks 93; Williams 24.

[81]The black plaintiff, Homer Plessy, sat in the "whites only" passenger car while travelling by train. When he was ordered to leave the car, he refused to move. Consequently, Plessy was removed from the train by police and arrested. As a result, he sued the railroad, arguing that segregated public facilities were illegal; See *Plessy v. Ferguson*, 16 S.Ct. 1138 and 163 U.S. 537, 1896; Brooks 88-89; Williams 9-10.

[82]Williams 92-93.

[83]Williams 95.

[84]Williams 96-97.

[85]Williams 99-100.

[86]Williams 102.

[87]Williams 103.

[88]Williams 106-107.

[89]Williams 112.

[90]Although the boycott disrupted the operation of the bus company for a week, black leaders accepted an offer from white bus and city officials. The offer stipulated fewer front seats (three) reserved for whites and all remaining seats filled on a first come first served basis with whites loading and sitting front to back and blacks loading and sitting back to front; See Morris 18-19, 24-25; Williams 60.

[91]Howell Raines, *My Soul is Rested: Movement Days in the Deep South Remembered* (New York: Putnam, 1977) 40; Brooks 94; Abernathy 133-136, 159, 160-161; Williams 61, 66-67, 88-89.

[92]The four students were: David Richmond, Franklin McCain, Ezell Blair, and Joseph McNeil; See Williams 128.

[93]U.S. Commission 107, 108; Raines 618.

[94]Williams 127-129.

[95]Brooks 62, 64; Williams 144-145, 147.

[96]Williams 147-149; Raines 122.

[97]Williams 147-149, 151, 153-155, 157-159; Raines 122.

[98]Williams 179, 181.

[99]Abernathy 241, 243; Raines 154; Williams 182, 193.

[100]Abernathy 250; Raines 154.

[101]Abernathy 262.

[102]According to Juan Williams, Connor had school buses brought in which transported 959 children to jail; See Williams 190.

[103]"Dogs and Hoses Used to Stall Negro Trek at Birmingham" *Atlanta Constitution* 4 May 1963, 1.

[104]Abernathy 268-269; Williams 193.

[105]Abernathy 270; "Troops are Sent to Alabama Bases in Wake of Birmingham Rioting" *Atlanta Constitution* 13 May 1963, 1.

[106]Williams 194.

[107]Brooks 21, 26-28; Williams 197-199; According to Williams, of the 250,000 participants in the March, at least 60,000 were white.

[108]Brooks 31; Williams 197-199.

[109]Abernathy 280-281.

[110]David Garrow, *Bearing the Cross: Martin Luther King, Jr. and the Southern Christian Leadership Conference* (New York: Random House, 1988) 337-338, 354-355.

[111]Williams 252.

[112]Williams 255, 258.

[113]Abernathy 298; Williams 255.

[114]Abernathy 297-298.

[115]Williams 265.

[116]Abernathy 350; Williams 267.

[117]Williams 273; Garrow 394-400; Abernathy 330-344.

[118]Abernathy 354, 359; Raines 216; Williams 282.

[119]Williams 278.

[120]I.F. Stone, "The Ultimate Stakes in the Voting Rights Struggle,: *I.F. Stone's Weekly* 22 March 1965, 1; Williams 278.

[121]Abernathy 497; Brooks 259; Kenneth O'Reilly, *Racial Matters : The FBI's Secret File on Black America, 1960-1972* (New York: Macmillan, 1989) 293; Williams 287.

[122]According to *Ebony* magazine, between 1957 and 1968 at least 40 black and white people, and countless unknown people, were killed in violence related to the civil rights struggle. In addition to the heretofore mentioned well-publicized deaths, they list lesser-known killings. See "Remembering the Martyrs of the Movement," *Ebony* Feb. 1990: 58, 60, 62.

[123]Abernathy 614; Williams 221.

[124]Abernathy 614; Williams 234-235.

[125]Abernathy 360, 614.

[126]Abernathy 360, 614.

[127]Abernathy 360, 614.

[128]Abernathy 416, 440-441; Williams 289.

[129]Taylor Branch, *Parting the Water: America in the King Years, 1954-1963* (New York: Simon and Schuster, 1988) 297, 922; Garrow 623-624.

[130]Abernathy 385, 358; Branch 21, 124-125; Garrow 15, 59, 287, 337, 599; Williams 29-35, 198, 282; Joseph Alvarez, *From Reconstruction to revolution: The Black's Struggle for Equality* (New York: Atheneum, 1971) 103.

Appendix B

Selected Golden Contemporaries

Although Golden was one of the most well-known and influential journalistic civil rights advocates, he found comfort, support, and inspiration in knowing that he was not alone.[1] Golden believed that some of his journalistic contemporaries (several Southern white journalists) "did much to encourage the social revolution of the American Negro."[2]

Like Golden, his journalistic contemporaries also attempted to eliminate southern racism and facilitate racial understanding. Each in his own way pointed out the evil of racism and the inequality of segregation while risking economic and physical harm. In addition, they denounced violence and promoted the concept of a peaceful and fair American society.

The background and advocacy of four of Golden's contemporaries, whom he considered friends, is briefly examined here. They include: Harry Ashmore, the executive editor of the *Arkansas Gazette*; Ralph McGill, the editor and publisher of the *Atlanta Constitution*; Percy Dale East, the owner/publisher/editor of the *Petal Paper*; and William Hodding Carter, Jr., the owner/publisher/ editor of the *Greenville Delta Democrat-Times*.[3]

Ashmore

Harry Ashmore considered Harry Golden a "gifted" and "highly effective civil rights advocate," who through an "irrepressible witty running commentary" in the *Carolina Israelite* "gently ridiculed preposterous manifestations of white supremacy" and helped to "Undermine resistance to desegregation."[4] Unlike the satiric and humorous personal journalism produced in North Carolina by Golden, Harry Ashmore produced straightforward non-humorous stories and editorials for a large Arkansas newspaper. Also unlike Golden, Ashmore was born and raised in the South. Throughout his career, Ashmore received numerous journalism awards and honors, including a Pulitzer Prize for distinguished editorial writing concerning civil rights during the 1957 "Little Rock Nine" crisis.[5]

Harry Ashmore's civil rights advocacy stemmed from his youth and life in the South, based upon which he arrived at the conclusion that he could not afford to ignore the problems of blacks. Ashmore believed that avoidance of blacks by whites would compound racial problems.[6] He also believed that blacks should be treated equally to whites. In addition, it was Ashmore's opinion that blacks were forcefully subjugated by whites who, from slavery to segregation, fashioned racist philosophies and restrictive social devices--laws, institutions.[7] Ashmore was aware of the severity and complexity of racism. He was also aware that potential problems could have arisen from the "polar attitudes" of whites "who do not accept Negroes as equals," and blacks "who are no longer satisfied with anything less [than equality]."[8] Nonetheless, Ashmore believed that no problem was beyond resolution by reasonable people.

Ashmore maintained that journalism could facilitate the process of attaining racial equality by serving as a "two-way bridge between the world of ideas and the world of men."[9] His ideals and civil rights advocacy are exemplified by his editorial writing during the Little Rock Nine crisis. Arkansas governor Orval Faubas resisted court-ordered school integration and ordered the Arkansas National Guard to take over the building and grounds of Central High School, thus keeping blacks from attending the school. Ashmore responded with a front-page editorial that challenged the governor's decision. On September 7, 1957, in the *Arkansas Gazette*, Ashmore wrote:

> [T]he issue is no longer segregation v. integration. The question has now become the supremacy of the United States in all matters of law. And clearly the federal government cannot let this issue remain unresolved no matter what the cost to the community.[10]
>
> [I]f Mr. Faubas in fact has no intention of defying federal authority now is the time for him to call a halt to the resistance which is preventing the carrying out of a duly entered court order. And certainly he should do so before his own actions become the cause of the violence he professes to fear.[11]

McGill

Ralph McGill was "entranced" by Golden's writing and considered him a "sage and philosopher."[12] McGill also occasionally used satire, Golden's dominant form, when writing about bigotry and racial inequality.[13] As a major civil rights advocate in Georgia and the South, McGill, like

Golden, began to write about southern race relations during the early 1940s.[14] However, unlike Golden, McGill spent most of his career at a large city newspaper, the *Atlanta Constitution.*

After starting as the sports editor with the *Constitution* in 1929, McGill worked his way up to editor by 1942, and publisher by 1960.[15] He considered racial segregation and discrimination a curse endured by the South and believed that as long as white southerners were preoccupied with denying blacks advancement and opportunity, blacks would never enter the mainstream of American society.[16] Therefore, between the 1940s and the 1960s, McGill advocated civil rights for blacks in the pages of the *Constitution* by addressing racial hatred, violence, discrimination, and the wrongs of segregation. In doing so, he wrote about the rights of blacks at a time when many southern whites remained silent or hostile to changes in black social status.[17] Some white readers of the *Constitution* were offended by his civil rights stance. Consequently, McGill was regularly threatened, occasionally attacked, and generally hated by some southern whites.[18] Despite the unpopularity of McGill's civil rights stance, in parts of the white community, he believed that all free individuals had a moral responsibility to work toward the creation of a better world and oppose wrong even though it could lead to misunderstanding and criticism.[19] He also believed that blacks, in particular, "should not give up the struggle" for their rights.[20]

McGill's unrelenting stance on civil rights led to a Pulitzer Prize for outstanding editorial writing that urged racial equality, among numerous other awards.[21] His civil rights advocacy is exemplified by an *Atlanta Constitution* editorial concerning the assassination of Dr. Martin Luther King, Jr. After the 1968 assassination of Dr. King in Memphis, Tennessee, McGill wrote:

> White slaves killed Dr. King. The moment the trigger man fired, King was the free man. The white killer was a slave to fear, a slave to his own sense of inferiority, a slave to hatred, a slave to all the bloody instincts that surge in a brain when a human being decides to become a beast. The Memphis killer and his associates have done their own race a grave and hideous injustice. They have elected the beast in man. [I]t is perhaps too much to hope, but much of the violent reaction to this bloody murder could be blunted if in every city and town there would now be a resolve to remove what remains of injustice and racial prejudice from schools, from training and job opportunities, from housing and community life in general. If injustice and inequity, if racist prejudices and discriminations now become the targets of all decent men and women, Dr. King's death may bring about what he sought for himself, his people, and his country.[22]

East

P.D. East admired Harry Golden and considered Golden's work as an asset to the struggle for civil rights.[23] As a personal journalist who utilized satire to attack racism,[24] East was more similar in style to Golden than were Ashmore and McGill. However, East, unlike Golden, Ashmore, or McGill, incorporated the use of mock notices and advertisements in his satire. Like Ashmore and McGill and unlike Golden, East was born and raised in the South--Columbia, Mississippi.[25] As a young adult, he decided to start his own small town southern newspaper. With the founding of the *Petal Paper* in 1953, East realized his ambition of newspaper ownership and began putting out a paper that was initially devoted to features and local news from Petal, Mississippi[26] and, according to East, "designed to keep everyone happy."[27] In the fall of 1954, when the Mississippi state legislature considered abolishing the state's public school system in order to avoid integration, East decided to risk the peace of his non-controversial newspaper by taking a stand on the school integration issue. Based on his belief that blacks were equal to whites, like Ashmore, and also on his belief in the United States Constitution, East editorialized against the proposed action of the legislature and began regularly attacking racism through the paper. As a result, within five years he lost all of his local circulation and advertising.[28]

Surviving primarily on national advertising and circulation, and some international circulation, East continued to attack racism through the *Petal Paper*. Consequently, he started receiving threatening telephone calls, obscene letters, and in-person threats of violence. Harassment and threats of violence escalated to such an extent that East, fearing for his life and well-being, relocated the paper from Mississippi to Alabama.[29]

Among the targets of East's intense satire were white supremacy organizations like the Ku Klux Klan and the various White Citizens Councils. In March of 1956, East learned of plans for the organization of a branch of the White Citizens Council in his community. He opposed the formation of the group by running a full-page notice that proclaimed:

Yes, you too can be Superior,
Join the Citizens Clan and
Be Safe From Social Worries.
Be Super-Superior.[30]

The notice went on to list the benefits of membership, including:

-Freedom to interpret the Constitution to your own personal advantage,
-Freedom to yell 'Nigger' as much as you please without your conscience bothering you,
-Freedom to take a part in the South's fastest growing business, Bigotry, and
-Freedom to be superior without brain, character, or principle.[31]

Carter

Through his paper, the *Greenville Delta Democrat-Times*, Hodding Carter commented on the "southern scene," and fought for civil justice against racial injustice in the late 1940s and 1950s.[32] In 1932, during his earlier journalism career, Carter was fired from his position as a reporter for the Associated Press in New Orleans. At that time, his employer also informed him that he "would never make a newspaperman."[33] Carter ignored this setback in his career and vowed never to work for anyone else again. Subsequently, he returned to his hometown of Hammond, Louisiana, and within the same year started his own paper, the *Hammond Daily Courier*.[34]

Having been born and raised in the South, like Ashmore, McGill, and East, Carter gained a first-hand perspective on southern race relations. Images from his early twentieth century Louisiana upbringing, such as his recurring vision of "a Negro woman dangling from a tree the morning after a mob had lynched her,"[35] later served to influence his thinking and writing about racism. Carter believed that patterns of racism, violence, and inequality were the central reasons for the social, political, and moral conflicts of the South.[36] In addition, he considered it ironic that the agricultural economy of the South was built "on the back of unskilled black men."[37] Yet, blacks remained "unassimilated and unassimilable" in the South.[38]

Carter's civil right writing was also shaped by his relocation to Greenville, Mississippi. He moved to Greenville at the age of 29, at the invitation of the Greenville business community, where he bought and began to operate the *Delta Democrat-Times* as the only daily paper.[39] As was the case with Golden, Ashmore, McGill, and East, many whites came to consider Carter controversial because of his pro-civil rights editorial stance. Carter's advocacy is exemplified by his comments on the treatment of civil rights workers by southern policemen:

> With monotonous regularity civil rights activists in Mississippi claim they have been beaten either by law officers or prisoners bribed by the officers to attack them in various jails. . . . The midnight beating and the old-fashioned third degree are still too prevalent, especially where Negroes and civil rights 'outsiders' are concerned. While all-white Mississippi juries have refused to convict lawmen in several trials involving beatings, the evidence has been incontrovertible that the beatings occurred. It is more than a coincidence that the only prisoners who are consistently coming out of jail with bruises and black eyes are civil rights activists. This isn't law. It is sadism hiding behind a badge.[40]

Carter was regularly harassed because of his outspokenness. On many occasions, he received anonymous threatening and obscene telephone calls and letters.[41] According to Carter, some letters suggested that: he was "a nigger-loving yankee communist who advocated the mongrelization of the [white] race; his home was a "haven for visiting subversives from Europe, Africa, Asia, and New York City; the *Delta Democrat-Times* was "owned by a millionaire northern Negro" who used Carter as a "mouthpiece"; and the *Delta Democrat-Times* office was the "secret headquarters of the NAACP."[42]

Carter's harassment was not limited to anonymous telephone calls and letters. In 1955, after editorializing against the formation of White Citizens Councils in Mississippi, as did East, the Mississippi state legislature passed a resolution declaring Carter "a writer of falsehoods."[43]

The controversy surrounding the Citizen Councils eventually contributed to a loss of advertising revenue for the *Delta Democrat-Times*. Despite the financial setback, Carter continued to successfully operate the paper.[44]

The work of individual journalists like Harry Golden, Harry Ashmore, Ralph McGill, P.D. East, and Hodding Carter served to complement and facilitate the work and accomplishments of civil rights leaders, organizations, and workers. Despite the risk of economic and violent repercussions, these journalistic civil rights advocates actively sought and encouraged right over wrong during a time when speaking out against racism was unpopular. In the process, discussion of the race issue was kept before the white audiences, blacks were provided with encouragement, and racial understanding and acceptance were aided.

Appendix B Notes

[1]Harry Golden, "Negro Intellectuals and White Liberals," *Congress Bi-Weekly* 15 Nov. 1965: 11.

[2]Harry Golden, *Mr. Kennedy and the Negroes* (Cleveland: World, 1964) 48.

[3]In addition to Golden and McGill, Dr. Martin Luther King, Jr. also gave credit to Lillian Smith and James Dabbs as significant white journalists who were advocates of civil rights and racial equality (See Chapter 3, Note# 20).

[4]Harry Ashmore, *Hearts and Minds: The Anatomy of Racism from Roosevelt to Reagan* (New York: McGraw-Hill, 1982) 100-102; Harry Ashmore, letter to Harry Golden, 25 May 1966, Box 13 File 20, Harry Golden Collection Part II, U of North Carolina at Charlotte.

[5]Harry Ashmore, *The Other Side of Jordan* (New York: Norton, 1960) 9; Harry Ashmore, *The Man in the Middle* (Columbia: The University of Missouri Press,1966) v; Williams, *Eyes* 104.

[6]Ashmore, *Other Side* 9.

[7]Ashmore, *Other Side* 10; Ashmore, *Man* 27.

[8]Harry Ashmore, *The Negro and the School* (Chapel Hill: The University of North Carolina Press, 1954) xv.

[9]Ashmore, *The Negro* xv.

[10]Ashmore, *Hearts* 259.

[11]Ashmore, *Hearts* 259.

[12]Ralph McGill, letter to Harry Golden, 6 Jan. 1958, Box 13 File 20, Harry Golden Collection Part II, U of North Carolina at Charlotte; Ralph McGill, *No Place to Hide: The South and Human Rights* ed. C.M. Logue (Macon: Mercer, University Press, 1984) 267.

[13]McGill, *No Place* xxvi; Michael Strickland, Harry Davis, and Jeff Strickland, *The Best of Ralph McGill* (Atlanta: Cherokee, 1980) xxii.

[14]Taylor Branch, *Parting the Waters: America in the King Years, 1954-63* (New York: Simon and Schuster, 1988) 66, 857; Strickland, et al. xxii; Eugene Patterson, interview, *My Soul is Rested: Movement Days in the Deep South Remembered* Howell Raines (New York: Putnam, 1977) 367.

[15]Ralph McGill, *The South and the Southerner* (Boston: Little and Brown, 1964) 130; Strickland, et al. xvii.

[16]Ralph McGill, *Southern Encounters: Southerners of Note in Ralph McGill's South* ed. C.M. Logue (Macon: Mercer University Press, 1983) 9; McGill, *No Place* 134-140; Strickland, et al. xxi, xvi.

[17]McGill, *No Place* xxvi, xliii; Eugene Patterson, interview, *My Soul is Rested: Movement Days in the Deep South Remembered* Howell Raines (New York: Putnam, 1977) 367-368.

[18]McGill, *No Place* 648.

[19]McGill, *Southern Encounters* 4.

[20]McGill, *No Place* 653.

[21]McGill, *No Place* 648; Strickland, et al. xviii; Eugene Patterson, interview, *My Soul is Rested: Movement Days in the Deep South Remembered* Howell Raines (New York: Putnam, 1977) 367.

[22]Ralph McGill, "A Free Man was Killed by White Slaves," *Atlanta Constitution* 5 April 1968: 1.

[23]P.D. East, letter to Harry Golden, 19 Feb. 1962, Box 6 File 15, Harry Golden Collection Part II, U of North Carolina at Charlotte; William Goldhurst, Telephone interview. 28 Oct. 1989.

[24]P.D. East, *The Magnolia Jungle: The Life Times and Education of a Southern Editor* (New York: Simon and Schuster, 1960) ix; William Goldhurst, "Death of Southern Editor Recalls Early Struggle," *Petal Paper* April 1972: 4.

[25]P.D. East, "Notes from a Southern Editor," *Black, White, and Gray* ed. Daniel Bradford (New York: Libraries, 1964) 128.

[26]East, *Magnolia* 121; P.D. East, "The Case of the Petal Paper" *New York Times* 28 July 1971: 35; P.D. East, "The Easy Chair" *Harper's* 19 Feb. 1959: 13-18; Goldhurst, *Death of* 4.

[27]East, *Magnolia* 121.

[28]East *The Case* 35; East, *The Easy Chair* 13; Harry Golden, "P.D. East of the Mississippi," *Carolina Israelite* Dec. 1956: 15.

[29]East, *The Case* 35; East *The Easy Chair* 18; Goldhurst, *Death of* 4; Harry Golden, *So Long as You're Healthy* (New York: Putnam, 1970) 239-240.

[30]East, *The Easy Chair* 16; East, *Magnolia* 176-177.

[31]East, *Magnolia* 177.

[32]Hodding Carter, *First Person Rural* (New York: Doubleday, 1963) 8; Bruce Garrison, "William Hodding Carter Jr.: A Different Perspective of the Crusading Editor," *Journalism History* 3.3 (1976): 90.

[33]Hodding Carter, *Where Main Street Meets the River* (New York: Rinehart, 1952) 1.

[34]Garrison 90; Carter, *Where Main* 5.

[35]Carter, *Where Main* 228.

[36]Carter, *First Person* 60.

[37]Carter, *First Person* 60.

[38]Carter, *First Person* 58.

[39]Carter, *First Person* 232.

[40]Hodding Carter, Editorial *The Trouble I've Seen: White Journalist/Black Movement* Paul Good (Washington, D.C.: Howard U P, 1975) 119.

[41]Carter, *First Person* 232; Garrison 90.

[42]Carter, *First Person* 233-234.

[43]Hodding Carter, "Liar by Legislation," *Look* June 1965: 32-36.

[44]Garrison 92, 96.

BIBLIOGRAPHY

Books and Pamphlets

Abernathy, Ralph David. *And the Walls Came Tumbling Down.* New York: Harper and Row, 1989.

Alvarez, Joseph. *From Reconstruction to Revolution: The Black Struggle for Equality.* New York: Atheneum, 1971.

Ashmore, Harry. *Hearts and Minds: The Anatomy of Racism from Roosevelt to Reagan.* New York: McGraw-Hill, 1982.

---*The Man in the Middle.* Columbia: U of Missouri P, 1966.

---*The Negro and the School.* Chapel Hill: U of North Carolina P, 1954.

---*The Other Side of Jordan.* New York:Norton, 1960.

Barzun, Jacques, and Henry Graff. *The Modern Researcher.* 4th ed. New York: Harcourt Brace Jovanovich, 1985.

Black, Jay and Frederick Whitney. *Mass Communication.* Dubuque: Brown, 1983.

Bradford, Daniel, ed. *Black White and Gray.* New York: Libraries, 1964.

Branch, Taylor. *Parting the Waters: America in the King Years, 1954-63.* New York: Simon and Schuster, 1988.

Brooks, Thomas. *Walls Come Tumbling Down: A History of the Civil Rights Movement, 1940-1970.* Englewood Cliffs: Prentice-Hall, 1974. Camejo, Peter. *Racism, Revolution, Reaction, 1861-1877.* New York: Monad, 1967.

Carter, Hodding. *First Person Rural.* New York: Doubleday, 1963.

---*Where Main Street Meets the River*. New York: Rinehart, 1952.

Conlin, Joseph, ed. *The American Radical Press: 1880-1960*. 2 Vols. Westport: Greenwood, 1974.

Commission on Freedom of the Press. *A Free and Responsible Press*. Chicago: U of Chicago P, 1947.

Cox, LaWanda and John Cox, eds. *Reconstruction: the Negro, and the New South*. Columbia: U of South Carolina P, 1973.

Craven, Avery. *Reconstruction: The Ending of the Civil War*. New York: Holt, Rinehart, and Winston, 1969.

Dabbs, James. *Haunted by God*. Richmond: Knox, 1972.

---*Southern Heritage*. New York: Knopf, 1958.

Daniel, Bradford. *Black, White, and Gray: Twenty-One Points of View on the Race Question*. New York: Libraries, 1964.

Davis, Lenwood G. *Black-Jewish Relations in the United States, 1752-1984*. Westport: Greenwood, 1984.

De Fleur, Melvin and Sandra Ball Rokeach. *Theories of Mass Communication*. 4th ed. New York: Longman, 1982.

Dennis, Everette. *The Magic Writing Machine*. Eugene: U of Oregon, 1971.

Dennis, Everette and John Merrill. *Basic Issues in Mass Communications*. New York: Macmillan, 1984.

Douglas, William O. *Go East, Young Man*. New York: Vintage, 1974.

Dubois, W.E. Burghardt. *Black Reconstruction in America: An Essay Toward a History of the Part Which Black Folk Played in the Attempt to Reconstruct Democracy in America, 1860-1880*. New York: Russell and Russell, 1935.

East, P.D. *Editorial Reprints from the Petal Paper*. Petal: East, 1959.

---*The Magnolia Jungle: The Life Times and Education of a Southern Editor*. New York: Simon and Schuster, 1960.

Emery, Edwin and Michael Emery. *The Press and America: An Interpretive History of the Mass Media*. 5th ed. Englewood Cliffs: Prentice-Hall, 1984.

Emery, Edwin and Henry Smith. *The Press and America*. New York: Prentice-Hall, 1954.

Fisher, Paul and Ralph Lowenstein, eds. *Race and the News Media*. New York: Praeger, 1967.

Flippen, Charles. *Liberating the Media: The New Journalism*, Washington, D.C.: Acropolis, 1974.

Franklin, John Hope. *Reconstruction: After the Civil War*. Chicago: U of Chicago P, 1961.

Garrow, David. *Bearing the Cross: Martin Luther King, Jr. and the Southern Christian Leadership Conference*. New York: Vintage, 1988.

Glessing, Robert. *The Underground Press in America*. Bloomington: Indiana UP, 1970.

Golden, Harry. *The Best of Harry Golden*. Cleveland: World, 1967.

---*Book of Jewish Humor*. New York: Putnam, 1972.

---*Enjoy! Enjoy!* Cleveland: World, 1960.

---*Ess, Ess Mein Kindt*. New York: Putnam, 1966.

---*For 2 Cents Plain*. Cleveland: World, 1958.

---*Forgotten Pioneer*. Cleveland: World, 1963.

---*The Golden Book of Jewish Humor*. New York: Putnam, 1972.

---*The Greatest Jewish City in the World*. Garden City: Doubleday, 1972.

---*Harry Golden on Various Matters*. New York: Anti Defamation League of B'nai B'rith, 1966.

---*The Israelis*. New York: Putnam, 1971.

---*Jews in American History*. Charlotte: Martin, 1950.

---*Long Live Columbus*. New York: Putnam, 1975.

---*Mr. Kennedy and the Negroes*. Cleveland: World, 1964.

---*Only in America*. Cleveland: World, 1958.

---*Our Southern Landsman*. New York: Putnam, 1974.

---*The Right Time: An Autobiography by Harry Golden*. New York: Putnam, 1969.

---*So Long as You're Healthy*. New York: Putnam, 1970.

---*So What Else is New?* New York: Putnam, 1964.

---*Travels Through Jewish America*. Garden City: Doubleday, 1973.

---*You're Entitle'*. Cleveland: World, 1962.

Good, Paul. *The Trouble I've Seen*. Washington, D.C.: Howard UP, 1975.

Haldeman-Julius, Emanuel. *America's Fakirs and Guides*. Little Blue Book Series 1288. Girard: Haldeman-Julius, 1928.

---*The First Hundred Million*. New York: Simon and Schuster, 1928.

Halpern, Ben. *Jews and Blacks*. New York: Herder and Herder, 1971.

Hedebro, Goran. *Communication and Social Change in Developing Nations*. Ames: Iowa State UP, 1982.

Horton, Paul. *The Sociology of Social Problems*. 5th ed. Englewood Cliffs: Prentice-Hall, 1974.

Kessler, Lauren. *The Dissident Press: Alternative Journalism in American History*. Beverly Hills: Sage, 1984.

King, Martin Luther, Jr. *Letter from Birmingham City Jail*. Birmingham: American Friends Service Committee, 1963.

King, Wendell. *Social Movements in the United States*. New York: Random House, 1956.

Martindale, Carolyn. *The White Press and Black America*. New York: Greenwood, 1986.

McGill, Ralph. *No Place to Hide: The South and Human Rights*. Ed. C.M. Logue. Macon: Mercer UP, 1984.

---*The South and the Southerner*. Boston: Little and Brown, 1964.

---*Southern Encounters: Southerners of Note in Ralph McGill's South*. Ed. C.N. Logue. Macon: Mercer UP, 1989.

Metzker, Isaac. *A Bintel Brief*. New York: Ballantine, 1971.

Mordell, Albert. *The World of Haldeman-Julius*. New York: Twayne, 1960.

Morris, Aldon. *The Origins of the Civil Rights Movement: Black Communities Organizing for a Change*. New York: Macmillan, 1984.

O'Reilly, Kenneth. *Racial Matters: The FBI's Secret File on Black America, 1960-1972*. New York: Macmillan, 1989.

Payne, George. *History of Journalism in the United States*. New York: Appleton, 1926.

Pickett, Calder M. *Voices of the Past: Key Documents in the History of American Journalism*. Columbus: Grid,1977.

Pinkney, Alphonso. *The Committed*. New Haven: College and University, 1968.

Raines, Howell. *My Soul is Rested: Movement Days in the Deep South Remembered*. New York: Putnam, 1977.

Rivers, William, Theodore Peterson, and Jay Jensen. *The Mass Media and Modern Society*. 2nd ed. New York: Holt, Rinehart, and Winston, 1971.

Shafer, Robert, ed. *A Guide to Historical Method*. 3rd ed. Homewood: Dorsey, 1980.

Siebert, Fred, Theodore Peterson, and Wilbur Schramm. *Four Theories of the Press*. Urbana: U of Illinois P, 1972.

Smith. Lillian. *Killers of the Dream*. New York: Norton, 1949.

---*Now is the Time*. New York: Viking, 1955.

Solomon, Gus. *The Jewish Role in the American Civil Rights Movement*. London: World Jewish Congress, 1967.

Startt, James and David Sloan. *Historical Methods in Mass Communication*. Hillsdale: Erlbaum, 1989.

Stone, I.F. *Polemics and Prophecies: 1967-1970*. New York: Random House, 1970.

Strickland, Michael, Harry Davis, and Jeff Strickland. *The Best of Ralph McGill*. Atlanta: Cherokee, 1980.

Suggs, Henry Lewis. *The Black Press in the South, 1965-1979*. Westport: Greenwood, 1983.

Tichenor, Phillip, George Donohue, and Clarice Olien. *Community Conflict and the Press*. Beverly Hills: Sage, 1980.

Warren, Robert Penn. *Who Speaks for the Negro*. New York: Random House, 1965.

White, David, ed. *Little Blue Books*. New York: Arno, 1974.

White House Conference: To Fulfill These Rights. Washington, D.C.: White House, 1966.

Williams, Juan. *Eyes on the Prize: America's Civil Rights Years*. New York: Penguin, 1988.

Portions of Books

Brechner, Joseph. "Were Broadcasters Color Blind." *Race and the News Media*. Eds. Paul Fisher and Ralph Lowenstein. New York: Praeger, 1967. 98-99.

Boone, Buford. "Southern Newsmen and Local Pressure." *Race and the News Media*. Eds. Paul Fisher and Ralph Lowenstein. New York: Praeger, 1967. 50.

Carter, Hodding. Editorial. *The Trouble I've Seen: White Journalist/Black Movement*. By Paul Good. Washington, D.C.: Howard U P, 1975. 119.

Dalsimer, Samuel. "The Justice of Persuasion." *Race and the News Media*. Eds. Paul Fisher and Ralph Lowenstein. New York: Praeger, 1967. 120.

Douglas, William O. Foreword. *The Best of Harry Golden*. by Harry Golden. Cleveland: World, 1967. ix.

East, P.D. "Notes from a Southern Editor." *Black, White, and Gray*. Ed. Daniel Bradford. New York: Libraries, 1964.

Fanning, Lawrence. "The Media: Observer or Participant?" *Race and the News Media*. Eds. Paul Fisher and Ralph Lowenstein. New York: Praeger, 1967. 110.

Farmer, Don. "Heat and Light through the TV Tube." *Race and the News Media*. Eds. Paul Fisher and Ralph Lowenstein. New York: Praeger, 1967. 74.

Golden, Harry. "1910's: Harry Golden." *Five Boyhoods*. Ed. Martin Levin. New York: Doubleday, 1962. 45.

---"Harry Golden." *Negro and Jews: An Encounter in America*. Ed. Shlomo Katz. New York: Macmillan, 1967, 64.

---Foreword. *A Bintel Brief*. By Isaac Metzker. New York: Ballantine, 1971, 1-11.

---Foreword. *The World of Haldeman-Julius*. By Albert Mordell. New York: Twayne, 1960. 5-7.

Howe, Irving. "Growing Up in the Ghetto." *World of Our Fathers*. New York: Simon and Schuster, 1976. 256-286.

---"The Yiddish Press." *World of Our Fathers*. New York: Simon and Schuster, 1976. 518-551.

Jensen, Jay. "The New Journalism in Historical Perspective." *Liberating the Media: The New Journalism*. Ed. Charles Flippen. Washington, D.C.: Acropolis, 1974. 18-28.

Klein, Woody. "The New Revolution: A Postscript." *Race and the News Media*. Eds. Paul Fisher and Ralph Lowenstein. New York: Praeger, 1967. 144.

Koop, Theodore. "Personal Journalism in Television." *Liberating the Media: The New Journalism*. Ed. Charles Flippen. Washington, D.C.: Acropolis, 1974. 145-151.

Monroe, William, Jr. "Television: The Chosen Instrument of the Revolution." *Race and the News Media*. Eds. Paul Fisher and Ralph Lowenstein. New York: Praeger, 1967. 97.

Moon, Henry. "Beyond Objectivity: The Fighting Press." *Race and the News Media.* Eds. Paul Fisher and Ralph Lowenstein. New York: Praeger, 1967. 134.

Peter, William. "The Visible and Invisible Images." *Race and the News Media*. Eds. Paul Fisher and Ralph Lowenstein. New York: Praeger, 1967. 81.

Poston, Ted. "The American Negro and Newspaper Myths." *Race and the News Media*. Eds. Paul Fisher and Ralph Lowenstein. New York: Praeger, 1967. 63.

Young, Thomas. "Voices of Protest, Prophecy of Change." *Race and the News Media*. Eds. Paul Fisher and Ralph Lowenstein. New York: Praeger, 1967. 125.

Articles

Barrow, Lionel, Jr. "Our Own Cause: Freedom's Journal and the Beginnings of the Black Press." *Journalism Quarterly* 4.4 (1977-78): 118-122.

Bennion, Sherilyn Cox. "Woman Suffrage Papers of the West, 1869-1914." *American Journalism* 3 (1986): 125-141.

Carter, Hodding. "Liar by Legislation." *Look* June 1965: 32-36.

---"Mississippi Legislature." Editorial. *Greenville Delta Democrat-Times* 3 April 1955: 1.

Cottrell, Robert. "I.F. Stone: A Maverick Journalist's Battle with the Superpowers." *Journalism History* 12.2 (1985): 62.

Crist, Judith. "Golden, Best Seller Author, Reveals his Prison Past." *New York Herald Tribune* 18 Sept. 1958: 1.

Dahrendorf, Ralf. "Toward a Theory of Social Conflict." *Journal of Conflict Resolution* 2.2 (1958): 178.

Dinnerstein, Leonard. "Southern Jewry and the Desegregation Crisis, 1954-1970." *American Jewish Historical Quarterly* 62 (1973): 231.

"Dogs and Hoses Used to Stall Negro Trek at Birmingham." *Atlanta Constitution* 4 May 1963, 1.

East, P.D. "The Case of the Petal Paper." *New York Times* 28 July 1971: 35.

---"The Easy Chair." *Harper's* 19 Feb. 1959: 13-18.

Emery, Michael. "The Writing of American Journalism History." *Journalism History* 10,3-4 (1983): 42.

"Five are Named to Hall of Fame." *JAFA News* April 1983: 1.

Garrison, Bruce. "William Hodding Carter, Jr.: A Different Perspective of the Crusading Editor." *Journalism History* 3.3 (1976): 90.

Gary, Kays. "Golden Pardoned for 1929 Crime." *Charlotte Observer* 7 Dec. 1973: 1a-2a.

Golden, Harry. "25th Anniversary." *Carolina Israelite* Nov.-Dec. 1966: 8.

---"1312 Elizabeth Avenue." *Carolina Israelite* Sept.-Oct. 1962: 6.

---"Alachua General Hospital." *Carolina Israelite* Jan.-Feb. 1962: 1.

---"The American Dream." *Johns Hopkins Magazine* April 1962: 36.

---"Another Modest Proposal." *Carolina Israelite* Jul.-Aug. 1962: 4.

---"Anti-Semitism." *Carolina Israelite* Feb. 1944: 4.

---"Black Power." *Carolina Israelite* Jul.-Aug. 1966: 2.

---"The Bull Connor Award." *Carolina Israelite* May-June 1963: 12.

---"The Carolina Israelite's Printing." *Carolina Israelite* Feb. 1957: 1.

---"Citation from Carver College." *Carolina Israelite* June 1966: 3.

---"Civil Rights for a Selfish Reason." *Carolina Israelite* April 1964: 9.

---"E. Haldeman-Julius--His Career and Personality." *American Freeman* Nov. 1951: 1.

---"Emanuel Haldeman-Julius." *Carolina Israelite* Jan.-Feb. 1968: 8.

---"Five Boyhoods." *Carolina Israelite* May-June 1962: 11.

---"Fighting Jews." *Carolina Israelite* Feb. 1944: 7.

---"The Future of Civil Rights." *Carolina Israelite* April-May 1976: 16.

---"Giving." *Carolina Israelite* Aug. 1956: 1.

---"The Golden Carry-the-Books Plan." *Carolina Israelite* Jan.-Feb. 1959: 7.

---"Golden Out-of-Order Plan in Operation." *Carolina Israelite* June 1958: 1.

---"The Golden Pogo Stick Plan." *Carolina Israelite* April 1959: 2.

---"The Golden Vertical Insurance Plan." *Carolina Israelite* Sept.-Oct. 1964: 15.

---"The Golden Vertical Negro Plan in Operation." *Carolina Israelite* Sept.- Oct. 1951: 1.

---"The Golden Vertical Plan in Reverse." *Carolina Israelite* Nov.-Dec. 1960: 18.
---"Goodbye." *Carolina Israelite* Jan.-Feb. 1968: 1, 2, 5.
---"Gradual Desegregation." *Carolina Israelite* Feb. 1957: 1.
---"Gradual Integration." *Carolina Israelite* May-June 1962: 10.
---"Haldeman-Julius--The Success that Failed." *Midstream: A Quarterly Jewish Review* 3.2 (1957): 28.
---"Hate Mail." *Carolina Israelite* May-June 1965: 1.
---"History of Jews in America." *Carolina Israelite* Feb. 1944: 8.
---"How About the Black Ink." *Carolina Israelite* May-June 1960: 24.
---"How to Solve the Segregation Problem." *Carolina Israelite* June 1956: 1.
---"How to Solve the Segregation Problem: The White Baby Plan." *Carolina Israelite* Mar.-Apr. 1957: 1.
---"Hysterical Audience." *Carolina Israelite* Jan.-Feb. 1962: 12.
---"Indoors--Vertical Negro, Outdoors-- Sittin' Down." *Carolina Israelite* May-June 1963: 1.
---"Integration and the Jews." *Carolina Israelite* Mar.-Apr. 1960: 7.
---"Jew and Gentile in the New South." *Commentary* Nov. 1955: 412.
---"Jewish Wit." *Carolina Israelite* Dec. 1965: 5.
---"Johnny Carson Show." *Carolina Israelite* May-June 1965: 1.
---"Let's Put it to the Test." *Carolina Israelite* Sept.-Oct. 1963: 16.
---"Letter to an Angry Jew." *Carolina Israelite* Sept.-Oct. 1960: 17.
---"A Matter of Human Dignity." *Integrator* Spring 1969: 4.
---"My Friend Emanuel." *American Freeman* Nov. 1955: 1.
---"My Critics." *Carolina Israelite* Jul.-Aug. 1965: 30.
---"My Testimony Before the Senate Committee." *Carolina Israelite* Nov.-Dec. 1966: 1.

---"My Turban Plan and Sir Fitzroy." *Carolina Israelite* Feb. 1962: 9.
---"The Need for a Low Man on the Totem Pole." *Carolina Israelite* Aug. 1958: 8.
---"The Negro Gives Us a Free Ride." *Carolina Israelite* Jul.-Aug. 1966: 14.
---"Negro Intellectuals and White Liberals." *Congress Bi-Weekly* 15 Nov. 1965: 11.
---"The Negro Maid and Protocol." *Carolina Israelite* Jan.-Feb. 1960: 14.
---"The Negro Protests." *Carolina Israelite* Jul.-Aug. 1963: 1.
---"Net Circulation." *Carolina Israelite* Oct. 1959: 12.
---"The New Drugs--An Easy End to Segregation." *Carolina Israelite* Mar.-Apr. 1961: 17.
---"A New Golden Plan to End Racial Segregation." *Carolina Israelite* Jul.-Aug. 1961: 1.
---"The New Man." *Carolina Israelite* Nov.-Dec. 1963: 13.
---"No One Here But Us Chickens." *Carolina Israelite* Nov.-Dec. 1961: 18.
---"P.D. East of Mississippi." *Carolina Israelite* Dec. 1956: 15.
---"The Peculiar Institution." *Carolina Israelite* Sept.-Oct. 1960: 6.
---"The Pickets are Getting 30 Days in Jail." *Carolina Israelite* Sept.-Oct. 1962: 12.
---"A Plan to End Racial Segregation." *Carolina Israelite* Aug. 1959: 11.
---"A Plan to Revive Motion Picture Business in the South." *Carolina Israelite* Feb. 1959: 5.
---"The President's Voting Proposals." *Carolina Israelite* Mar.-Apr. 1965: 7.
---"The Pressure on the Carolina Israelite." *Carolina Israelite* Oct. 1957: 4.
---"Racial Segregation." *Carolina Israelite* Aug. 1955: 5.
---"Readership." *Carolina Israelite* Mar.-Apr. 1959: 9.
---"The Revolution." *Carolina Israelite* Sept.-Oct. 1963: 4.
---"The Senate Hearing." *Carolina Israelite* Nov.-Dec. 1966: 8.

---"The Sit-in Demonstrations." *Carolina Israelite* Mar.-Apr. 1960: 5.

---"The Sit-ins Produced Some Excellent American Humor." *Carolina Israelite* Sept.-Oct. 1960: 2.

---"Smorgasbord is Running the Golden Vertical Plan." *Carolina Israelite* May-June 1961: 9.

---"Solve Race Problems and Revive Textiles." *Carolina Israelite* Aug, 1958: 3.

---"Southern Justice and the Negro." *Carolina Israelite* Nov.-Dec. 1965: 15.

---"The Topics of the Times." *Carolina Israelite* Dec. 1957: 11.

---"The Turban is a Very Big Thing." *Carolina Israelite* Aug. 1956: 8.

---"The Vertical Plan." *Carolina Israelite* Jul.-Aug. 1962: 8.

---"The Vertical Plan in Operation." *Carolina Israelite* Sept.-Oct. 1960: 9.

---"We are Color-Happy." *Carolina Israelite* Sept.-Oct. 1960: 12.

---"We are all Colorless." *Carolina Israelite* Dec. 1958: 1.

---"What is Black Power?" *Carolina Israelite* Nov.-Dec. 1966: 10-11.

---"What's Behind it All?" *Carolina Israelite* Aug. 1964: 4.

---"Why Didn't She Stay Home?" *Carolina Israelite* May-June 1965: 26.

"Golden Rule." *Time* 1 April 1957: 62.

"The Golden Story." *Time* 29 Sept. 1958: 72.

Goldhurst, William. "Death of Southern Editor Recalls Early Struggle." *Petal Paper* April 1972: 4.

---"My Father, Harry Golden." *Midstream* June-Jul. 1969: 68+.

Gunn, John. "My Friend Emanuel." *American Freeman* Nov. 1951: 1.

Haldeman-Julius, Emanuel. "Writers." *American Freeman* May 1951: 2.

"Harry Golden Lectureship." *UNC-C News* Summer 1969: 3.

Hohner, Robert. "The Other Harry Golden: Harry Goldhurst and the Cannon Scandals." *The North Carolina Historical Review* 65 (1988): 154-172.

Jensen, Jay. "Excerpt from the New Journalism in Historical Perspective." *Journalism History* 1.2 (1974): 37.

La Brie, Henk. "Black Newspapers: The Roots are 150 Years Deep." *Journalism History* 4.4 (1978-79): 111-113.

Lerner, Max. "The Secret Place." *New York Post* 21 Sept. 1958: M8.

"Little Blue Books." *Time* 15 Aug. 1960: 38-39.

McCombs, Malcolm, and Donald Shaw. "The Agenda-Setting Function of the Press." *Public Opinion Quarterly* 36 (1972): 176-187.

McGill, Ralph. "Bull Connor Helps Insight." *Atlanta Constitution* 14 May 1963: 1.

---"A Free Man Killed by White Slaves." *Atlanta Constitution* 5 April 1968: 1.

---"A Matter of Costs." *Atlanta Constitution* 9 May 1963: 1.

---"Nobel Prize Reminds Us." *Atlanta Constitution* 16 Oct. 1964: 1.

McKerns, Joseph. "The Limits of Progressive Journalism." *Journalism History* 4.3 (1977): 88.

Markowitz, Arnold. "Sense of Outrage Still Golden." *Miami Herald* 12 Mar. 1972: 6N.

Marvin, Carolyn. "Space, Time, and Captive Communication History." *Mass Communication Review Yearbook* 5 (1985): 111.

Mordell, Albert. "E. Haldeman-Julius--His Career and Personality." *American Freeman* Nov. 1951: 1.

"Remembering the Martyrs of the Movement." *Ebony* Feb. 1990: 58-62.

Ribalow, Harold. "Commentary vs. Harry Golden." *Congress Bi-Weekly* 13 Feb. 1961: 9-11.

Robinson, Douglas. "Harry Golden: On Things Remembered." *New York Times* 26 Feb. 1968: 36.

Rodgers, Harrell, Jr. "Civil Rights and the Myth of Popular Sovereignty." *Journal of Black Studies* 12.1 (1981): 56-57.

Saalberg, Harvey. "Bennett and Greeley, Professional Rivals, Had Much in Common." *Journalism Quarterly* 49.3 1972): 538-540.

Solotaroff, Theodore. "Harry Golden and the American Audience." *Commentary* Jan. 1961: 1-13.

Stone, I.F. "The Best Kept Secret of the Vietnam War." *I.F. Stone's Weekly* 4 April 1969: 1.

---"The Fear that Fuels the Arms Race." *I.F. Stone's Bi-Weekly* 4 Oct. 1971: 1.

---"The FBI's Indifference to Civil Rights." *I.F. Stone's Bi-Weekly* 14 Oct. 1963: 1.

---"McCarthy Falls Back on the Lunatic Fringe." *I.F. Stone's Weekly* 15 Nov. 1954: 1.

---"Notes on Closing, But Not in Farewell." *I.F. Stone's Bi-Weekly* n.d. Dec. 1971: 1.

---"The Right to Keep Other Beings 'Niggers.'" *I.F. Stone's Weekly* 24 Sept. 1956: 4.

---"The Senate Debate Through Negro Eyes." *I.F. Stone's Weekly* 29 Jul. 1957: 1.

---"The South Begins a Strategic Retreat." *I.F. Stone's Weekly* 9 Feb. 1959: 1.

---"Time for a Deportation to Wisconsin." *I.F. Stone's Weekly* 4 Apr. 1953: 2.

---"The Ultimate Stakes in the Voting Rights Struggle." *I.F. Stone's Weekly* 22 Mar. 1965: 1.

"Troops are Sent to Alabama Bases in Wake of Birmingham Rioting." *Atlanta Constitution* 13 May 1963: 1.

Webb, Joseph. "Historical Perspective on the New Journalism." *Journalism History* 1.2 (1974): 38.

Williams, Nudie. "Black Newspapers and the Exodusters of 1879." *Kansas History* 8 (1985-86): 217-225.

Research Paper, Thesis, Dissertation

Krause, Allen. "The Southern Rabbi and Civil Rights." Thesis. Hebrew Union College, 1967.

Teel, Leonard. "The Connemara Correspondents: Sandburg, Golden, and McGill." History Div., AEJMC Southeast Regional Colloquium. Chapel Hill, April 1989.

Thomas, Clarence. "The Journalistic Civil Rights Advocacy of Harry Golden and the *Carolina Israelite*". Dissertation. U of Florida, 1990.

Interviews

Bond, Julian. Personal interview. 7 Sept. 1994.

Brown, Anita. Telephone interview. 6 June 1990.

Farmer, James. Personal interview. 6 Jan. 1996

Golden Harry. Interview. *Sunday Morning* CBS TV 25 Oct. 1981.

Goldhurst, William. Personal interview. 30 Jan. 1990.

---Personal interview. 27 Feb. 1989.

---Personal interview. 28 Oct. 1989.

---Personal interview. 30 March 1990.

Hoffman, Wendell. Interview. *My Soul is Rested: Movement Days in the Deep South Remembered.* With Howell Raines. New York: Putnam, 1977. 377.

Lewis, John. Personal interview. 25 July 1994

Paterson, Eugene. Interview. *My Soul is Rested: Movement Days on the Deep South Remembered.* With Howell Raines. New York: Putnam, 1977. 367-368.

Smitherman, Joseph. Interview. *Eyes on the Prize: America's Civil Rights Years, 1954-1965.* With Juan Williams. New York: Penguin, 1988. 273.

Valeriani, Richard. Interview. *Eyes on the Prize: America's Civil Rights Years, 1954-1965*. With Juan Williams. New York: Penguin, 1988. 270.

Valeriani, Richard. Interview. *My Soul is Rested: Movement Days in the Deep South Remembered*. With Howell Raines. New York: Putnam, 1977. 371-372.

Vivian, C.T. Personal interview. 12 Aug. 1994.

Young, Andrew. Personal interview. 10 Aug. 1994.

Court Cases

Belton v. Gebhart from Delaware. 344 U.S. 891.

Bolling v. Sharpe from Washington, D.C. 347 U.S. 497, 74 S.Ct. 693.

Briggs v. Elliott from South Carolina 342 U.S. 350, 72 S.Ct. 327.

Browder v. Gayle 352 U.S. 903 and 202 F.Supp. 707.

Davis v. County School Board of Virginia. 103 F.Supp. 337.

Oliver Brown v. Board of Education of Topeka, Kansas. 75 S.Ct. 686.

Plessy v. Ferguson. 16 S.Ct. 1138 and 163 U.S. 537 1896.

Government Publications

Diggs, Charles. "How to Solve the Segregation Problem." *Congressional Record--Appendix*. U.S. House. Washington: GPO, 1957. A2832.

---"How to Solve the Segregation Problem--The White Baby Plan." *Congressional Record*. U.S. House. Washington: GPO, 1957. 5211.

Golden, Harry. "A 20th Century Committee of Correspondence." *Congressional Record*. U.S. House. Washington: GPO, 1966. 28328.

Hart, Philip. "The Importance of Education." *Congressional Record*. 89th Cong., 1st sess., Senate. Washington: GPO, 1965. 2833.

---"Race and Immigration." *Congressional Record*. Senate. 88th Cong., 1st sess., Senate. Washington: GPO, 1965. 22517.

Murray, James. "Charlotte's Harry Golden: Portrait of a Pleasant Myth." *Congressional Record--Appendix*. Senate. Washington: GPO, 1958. A2697.

Roosevelt, James. "The Golden Out-of-Order Plan in Operation." *Congressional Record--Appendix*. U.S. House. Washington: GPO, 1958. A6714.

United States. Commission on Civil Rights. *Civil Rights '63*. Washington: GPO, 1963.

---Cong. "Civil Rights Act of 1875." *United States Statutes at Large*. 44th Cong., Washington: GPO, 1875. 335.

---. ---. "Civil Rights Act of 1957." *United States Statutes at Large*. 88th Cong., Washington: GPO, 1958. 634.

---. ---. "Civil Rights Act of 1960." *United States Statutes at Large*. 86th Cong., Washington: GPO, 1961. 86+.

---. ---. "Civil Rights Act of 1964." *United States Statutes at Large*. 88th Cong., Washington: GPO, 1966. 241.

---. ---. "Civil Rights Act of 1968." *United States Statutes at Large*. 90th Cong., Washington: GPO, 1969. 83.

---. ---. "Voting Rights Act of 1965." *United States Statutes at Large*. 89th Cong., Washington: GPO, 1966. 538.

---House. Committee on the Judiciary. *School Busing*. U.S. 92nd Cong., 2nd sess., Washington: GPO, 1972, 641-644.

---Senate. Committee on Government Operations. Subcommittee on Executive Reorganization. *Federal Role in Urban Affairs*. 89th Cong., 2nd sess., Washington: GPO, 1966.

Weltner, Charles. "A 20th Century Committee of Correspondence." *Congressional Record*. 89th Cong., 2nd sess., U.S. House Washington: GPO, 1966. 28327.

Wilson, Harrison. "The South's Great Victory." *Congressional Record*. Senate. U.S. 88th Cong., 1st sess., Washington: GPO, 1963. 10589.

Album

Golden, Harry. *Golden Remembers* Vanguard VRS-9102, 1958.

Collections

Harry Golden Collection, Parts I and II, U of North Carolina at Charlotte, NC.

Harry Golden Collection, William Goldhurst Private Holdings, Gainesville, FL.

Letters

Alexander, Kelly M. Letter to Harry Golden. 26 Sept. 1960. Box 14 File 1. Harry Golden Collection Part II. U of North Carolina at Charlotte.

Anderson, William. Letter to Harry Golden. 15 Sept. 1971. Box 20 File 17. Harry Golden Collection Part II. U of North Carolina at Charlotte.

Anonymous Letter to World Publishing Company. 13 Sept. 1958. Box 32 File 285. Harry Golden Collection Part I. U of North Carolina at Charlotte.

Anonymous. Post Card to Harry Golden. 4 Aug. 1981. Box 2 File 12. Harry Golden Collection Part II. U of North Carolina at Charlotte.

Ashmore, Howard. Letter to Harry Golden. 25 May 1966. Box 11 File 20. Harry Golden Collection Part II. U of North Carolina at Charlotte.

Baker, Howard, Jr. Letter to Harry Golden. 24 Jan. 1978. Box 20 File 18. Harry Golden Collection Part II. U of North Carolina at Charlotte.

Bell, Holley. Letter to Harry Golden. 6 Dec. 1966. Box 20 File 14. Harry Golden Collection Part II. U of North Carolina at Charlotte.

Black, Hugo. Letter to Harry Golden. 1 Jul. 1963. Box 3 File 27. Harry Golden Collection Part II. U of North Carolina at Charlotte.

Black, Hugo. Letter to Harry Golden. 11 Dec. 1966. Box 3 File 27. Harry Golden Collection Part II. U of North Carolina at Charlotte.

Black, Hugo. Letter to Harry Golden. 18 Dec. 1968. Box 3 File 27. Harry Golden Collection Part II. U of North Carolina at Charlotte.

Black, Hugo. Letter to Harry Golden. 5 Mar. 1970. Box 3 File 27. Harry Golden Collection Part II. U of North Carolina at Charlotte.

Black, Hugo. Letter to Harry Golden. 26 Oct. 1970. Box 3 File 27. Harry Golden Collection Part II. U of North Carolina at Charlotte.

Bond, Mildred. Letter to Harry Golden. 4 Feb. 1959. Box 14 File 1. Harry Golden Collection Part II. U of North Carolina at Charlotte.

Bond, Mildred. Letter to Harry Golden. 22 May 1959. Box 14 File 1. Harry Golden Collection Part II. U of North Carolina at Charlotte.

Bond, Mildred. Letter to Harry Golden. 8 Sept. 1960. Box 14 File 1. Harry Golden Collection Part II. U of North Carolina at Charlotte.

Broyhill, James. Letter to Harry Golden. 22 Feb. 1973. Box 20 File 17. Harry Golden Collection Part II. U of North Carolina at Charlotte.

Buggs, John. Letter to Harry Golden. Jan. 1974. Box 5 File 14. Harry Golden Collection Part II. U of North Carolina at Charlotte.

Bunche, Ralph. Letter to Harry Golden. 30 Mar. 1964. Box 14 File 1. Harry Golden Collection Part II. U of North Carolina at Charlotte.

Bunche, Ralph. Letter to Harry Golden. 18 Mar. 1964. Box 14 File 1. Harry Golden Collection Part II. U of North Carolina at Charlotte.

Carter, Jimmy. Letter to Harry Golden. Mar. 1977. Box 4 File 22. Harry Golden Collection Part II. U of North Carolina at Charlotte.

Celler, Emanuel. Letter to Harry Golden. 19 Aug. 1965. Box 20 File 17. Harry Golden Collection Part II. U of North Carolina at Charlotte.

Church, Frank. Letter to Harry Golden. 18 Oct. 1961. Box 20 File 18. Harry Golden Collection Part II. U of North Carolina at Charlotte.

Cieplinski, Michael. Letter to Harry Golden. 12 Aug. 1964. Box 20 File 16. Harry Golden Collection Part II. U of North Carolina at Charlotte.

Clark, Joseph. Letter to Harry Golden. 9 Apr. 1963. Box 20 File 18. Harry Golden Collection Part II. U of North Carolina at Charlotte.

Corwin, Lloyd. Letter to Harry Golden. 12 Jan. 1977. Box 4 File 22. Harry Golden Collection Part II. U of North Carolina at Charlotte.

Craven, J. Braxton. Letter to Robert Wallace. 12 April 1971. Box 2 File 28. Harry Golden Collection Part II. U of North Carolina at Charlotte.

Culver, John. Letter to Harry Golden. 26 Nov. 1968. Box 20 File 17. Harry Golden Collection Part II. U of North Carolina at Charlotte.

Derounian, Steven. Letter to Harry Golden. 18 Aug. 1964. Box 20 File 17. Harry Golden Collection Part II. U of North Carolina at Charlotte.

Doar, John. Letter to Harry Golden. 10 Oct. 1963. Box 20 File 15. Harry Golden Collection Part II. U of North Carolina at Charlotte.

Dodd, Thomas. Letter to Harry Golden. 25 Nov. 1964. Box 20 File 18. Harry Golden Collection Part II. U of North Carolina at Charlotte.

Douglas, William O. Letter to Harry Golden. 1 Mar. 1968. Box 6 File 18. Harry Golden Collection Part II. U of North Carolina at Charlotte.

Douglas, William O. Letter to Harry Golden. 30 July 1969. Box 6 File 18. Harry Golden Collection Part II. U of North Carolina at Charlotte.

Drinan, Robert. Letter to Harry Golden. 6 May 1971. Box 20 File 17. Harry Golden Collection Part II. U of North Carolina at Charlotte.

Eagleton, Thomas. Letter to Harry Golden. 22 Aug. 1974. Box 30 File 18. Harry Golden Collection Part II. U of North Carolina at Charlotte.

East, P.D. Letter to Harry Golden. 19 Feb. 1962. Box 6 File 15. Harry Golden Collection Part II. U of North Carolina at Charlotte.

Eisenhower, Dwight. Letter to Harry Golden. 4 Dec. 1946. Box 6 File 35. Harry Golden Collection Part II. U of North Carolina at Charlotte.

Farbstein, Leonard. Letter to Harry Golden. 6 Jan. 1966. Box 20 File 17. Harry Golden Collection Part II. U of North Carolina at Charlotte.

Farmer, James. Letter to Harry Golden. 9 Jul. 1962. Box 19 File 30. Harry Golden Collection Part II. U of North Carolina at Charlotte.

Ford, Gerald. Letter to Harry Golden. 19 Aug. 1965. Box 7 File 23. Harry Golden Collection Part II. U of North Carolina at Charlotte.

Fountain, L.H. Letter to Harry Golden. 14 Feb. 1973. Box 20 File 17. Harry Golden Collection Part II. U of North Carolina at Charlotte.

Frankfurter, Felix. Letter to Harry Golden. 1 Jul. 1959. Box 32 File 686. Harry Golden Collection Part I. U of North Carolina at Charlotte.

Fraser, Donald. Letter to Harry Golden. 27 Jul. 1964. Box 20 File 17. Harry Golden Collection Part II. U of North Carolina at Charlotte.

Fretwell, E.K. Letter to Harry Golden, Jr. 2 Nov. 1981. Harry Golden Collection, William Goldhurst Private Holdings, Gainesville, FL.

Fulbright, J.W. Letter to Harry Golden. 19 Oct. 1961. Box 20 File 18. Harry Golden Collection Part II. U of North Carolina at Charlotte.

Galifianakis, Nick. Letter to Harry Golden. 22 June 1972. Box 20 File 17. Harry Golden Collection Part II. U of North Carolina at Charlotte.

Goldberg, Arthur. Letter to Harry Golden. 14 May 1964. Box 7 File 52. Harry Golden Collection Part II. U of North Carolina at Charlotte.

Golden, Harry. Letter to A. Phillip Randolph. 1 Sept. 1979. Box 17 File 10. Harry Golden Collection Part II. U of North Carolina at Charlotte.

Golden, Harry. Letter to Abraham Ribicoff. 19 Oct. 1966. Box 17 File 1. Harry Golden Collection Part II. U of North Carolina at Charlotte.

Golden, Harry. Letter to Agent in Charge FBI. 17 Mar. 1959. Box 7 File 11. Harry Golden Collection Part II. U of North Carolina at Charlotte.

Golden, Harry. Letter to Agent in Charge FBI. 30 Aug. 1962. Box 7 File 11. Harry Golden Collection Part II. U of North Carolina at Charlotte.

Golden, Harry. Letter to Arthur Goldburg. 10 Sept. 1962. Box 7 File 52. Harry Golden Collection Part II. U of North Carolina at Charlotte.

Golden, Harry. Letter to Charles Mantiband. 8 April 1960. Box 13 File 7. Harry Golden Collection Part II. U of North Carolina at Charlotte.

Golden, Harry. Letter to Harry Truman. 17 Feb. 1965. Box 19 File 64. Harry Golden Collection Part II. U of North Carolina at Charlotte.

Golden, Harry. Letter to Hubert H. Humphrey. 24 Mar. 1964. Box 10 File 38. Harry Golden Collection Part II. U of North Carolina at Charlotte.

Golden, Harry. Letter to M. Grusd. 30 Sept. 1951. Box 24 File 150. Harry Golden Collection Part II. U of North Carolina at Charlotte.

Golden, Harry. Letter to Martin Luther King, Jr. 17 Nov. 1965. Box 11 File 29. Harry Golden Collection Part II. U of North Carolina at Charlotte.

Golden, Harry. Letter to Newton Minow. 17 Sept. 1962. Harry Golden Collection Part II. U of North Carolina at Charlotte.

Golden, Harry. Letter to Rolfe Featherstone. 18 Aug. 1967. Box 19 File 30. Harry Golden Collection Part II. U of North Carolina at Charlotte.

Golden, Harry. Letter to William Goldhurst. 3 May 1977. Harry Golden Collection. William Goldhurst Private Holdings, Gainesville.

Golden, Harry. Letter to William O. Douglas. 11 Nov. 1974. Harry Golden Collection Part II. U of North Carolina at Charlotte.

Golden, Harry. Letter to William Ryan. 28 Jul. 1969. Box 8 File 27. Harry Golden Collection Part II. U of North Carolina at Charlotte.

Golden, Harry. Memorandum to Lyndon B. Johnson. 3 Sept. 1964. Harry Golden Collection. William Goldhurst Private Holdings, Gainesville, FL.

Golden, Harry. Telegram to Martin Luther King, Jr. 18 Mar. 1965. Box 11 File 29. Harry Golden Collection Part II. U of North Carolina at Charlotte.

Golden, Harry. Telegram to Martin Luther King, Jr. 15 Oct. 1964. Box 19 File 5. Harry Golden Collection Part II. U of North Carolina at Charlotte.

Graham, James A. Letter to Harry Golden. 3 Dec. 1979. Box 2 File 40. Harry Golden Collection Part II. U of North Carolina at Charlotte.

Gruening, Ernest. Letter to Harry Golden. 31 Jul. 1962. Box File 18. Harry Golden Collection Part II. U of North Carolina at Charlotte.

Halpern, Seymour. Letter to Harry Golden. 28 Mar. 1972. Box 20 File 17. Harry Golden Collection Part II. U of North Carolina at Charlotte.

Hart, Philip. Letter to Harry Golden 16 April 1969. Box 20 File 18. Harry Golden Collection Part II. U of North Carolina at Charlotte.

Harrington, Michael. Letter to Harry Golden. 9 Dec. 1975. Box 20 File 17. Harry Golden Collection Part II. U of North Carolina at Charlotte.

Hartke, Vance. Letter to Harry Golden. 31 Oct. 1974. Box 20 File 18. Harry Golden Collection Part II. U of North Carolina at Charlotte.

Heineman, Ben. Letter to Harry Golden. 14 May 1966. Box 10 File 37. Harry Golden Collection Part II. U of North Carolina at Charlotte.

Hollings, Ernest. Letter to Harry Golden. 3 Mar. 1969. Box 20 File 18. Harry Golden Collection Part II. U of North Carolina at Charlotte.

Holtzman, Elizabeth. Letter to Harry Golden. 27 Sept. 1974. Box 20 File 17. Harry Golden Collection Part II. U of North Carolina at Charlotte.

Howe, Harold. Letter to Harry Golden. 12 Dec. 1968. Box 20 File 13. Harry Golden Collection Part II. U of North Carolina at Charlotte.

Humphrey, Hubert H. Letter to Harry Golden. 21 Jan. 1960. Box 9 File 9. Harry Golden Collection Part II. U of North Carolina at Charlotte.

Humphrey, Hubert H. Letter to Harry Golden. 5 June 1962. Box 9 File 9. Harry Golden Collection Part II. U of North Carolina at Charlotte.

Humphrey, Hubert H. Letter to Harry Golden. 30 Aug. 1966. Box 9 File 9. Harry Golden Collection Part II. U of North Carolina at Charlotte.

Humphrey, Hubert H. Letter to Harry Golden. 4 Sept. 1964. Box 9 File 9. Harry Golden Collection Part II. U of North Carolina at Charlotte.

Humphrey, Hubert H. Letter to Harry Golden. 10 Sept. 1964. Box 10 File 38. Harry Golden Collection Part II. U of North Carolina at Charlotte.

Humphrey, Hubert H. Letter to Harry Golden. 30 June 1966. Box 9 File 9. Harry Golden Collection Part II. U of North Carolina at Charlotte.

Humphrey, Hubert H. Letter to Harry Golden. 23 Aug. 1968. Box 9 File 9. Harry Golden Collection Part II. U of North Carolina at Charlotte.

Javits, Jacob. Letter to Harry Golden. 30 July 1963. Box 10 File 8. Harry Golden Collection Part II. U of North Carolina at Charlotte.

Johnson, Lyndon B. Letter to Harry Golden. 2 Sept. 1960. Box 10 File 37. Harry Golden Collection Part II. U of North Carolina at Charlotte.

Johnson, Lyndon B. Letter to Harry Golden. 19 Aug. 1964. Box 10 File 38. Harry Golden Collection Part II. U of North Carolina at Charlotte.

Johnson, Lyndon B. Letter to Harry Golden. 29 Dec. 1964. Box 10 File 37. Harry Golden Collection Part II. U of North Carolina at Charlotte.

Johnson, Lyndon B. 15 June 1968. Box 10 File 37. Harry Golden Collection Part II. U of North Carolina at Charlotte.

Jonas, Charles. "Statement" at Harry Golden Day Luncheon. 19 May 1969. Harry Golden Collection. William Goldhurst Private Holdings, Gainesville, FL.

Jonas, Charles. Letter to Robert Wallace. 29 April 1969. Box 20 File 17. Harry Golden Collection Part II. U of North Carolina at Charlotte.

Joslyn, A.W. Letter to Harry Golden. 8 Jan. 1965. Box 20 File 17. Harry Golden Collection Part II. U of North Carolina at Charlotte.

Kennedy, Edward. Letter to Harry Golden. 4 Jan. 1967. Box 11 File 24. Harry Golden Collection Part II. U of North Carolina at Charlotte.

Kennedy, Edward. Letter to Harry Golden. 23 Sept. 1968. Box 11 File 24. Harry Golden Collection Part II. U of North Carolina at Charlotte.

Kennedy, Edward. Letter to Harry Golden. 6 Mar. 1970. Box 11 File 24. Harry Golden Collection Part II. U of North Carolina at Charlotte.

Kennedy, Edward. Letter to Harry Golden. 9 Dec. 1971. Box 11 File 24. Harry Golden Collection Part II. U of North Carolina at Charlotte.

Kennedy, Edward. Letter to Harry Golden. 20 Mar. 1973. Box 11 File 24. Harry Golden Collection Part II. U of North Carolina at Charlotte.

Kennedy, Edward. Letter to Harry Golden. 16 Oct. 1974. Box 11 File 24. Harry Golden Collection Part II. U of North Carolina at Charlotte.

Kennedy, Edward. Telegram to Harry Golden. 21 Nov. 1968. Box 11 File 24. Harry Golden Collection Part II. U of North Carolina at Charlotte.

Kennedy, Edward. Telegram to E.W. Colvard. 19 May 1969. Box 2 File 37. Harry Golden Collection Part II. U of North Carolina at Charlotte.

Kennedy, John F. Letter to Harry Golden. 13 Mar. 1959. Box 32 File 283. Harry Golden Collection Part I. U of North Carolina at Charlotte.

Kennedy, Robert. Letter to Harry Golden. 27 May 1959. Box 11 File 17. Harry Golden Collection Part II. U of North Carolina at Charlotte.

Kennedy, John F. Letter to Harry Golden. 29 Jul. 1959. Box 32 File 283. Harry Golden Collection Part I. U of North Carolina at Charlotte.

Kennedy, John F. Letter to Harry Golden. 20 Aug. 1960. Box 32 File 283. Harry Golden Collection Part I. U of North Carolina at Charlotte.

Kennedy, John F. Letter to Harry Golden. 17 Dec. 1960. Box 11 File 11. Harry Golden Collection Part II. U of North Carolina at Charlotte.

Kennedy, Mrs. John F. Letter to Harry Golden. 19 Jan. 1965. Harry Golden Collection. William Goldhurst Private Holdings, Gainesville.

Kennedy, John F. Invitation to Harry Golden. June 1966. Box 10 File 37. Harry Golden Collection Part II. U of North Carolina at Charlotte.

Kennedy, Robert. Letter to Harry Golden. 6 Nov. 1959. Box 11 File 17. Harry Golden Collection Part II. U of North Carolina at Charlotte.

Kennedy, Robert. Letter to Harry Golden. 22 June 1960. Box 11 File 17. Harry Golden Collection Part II. U of North Carolina at Charlotte.

Kennedy, Robert. Letter to Harry Golden. 29 July 1963. Box 11 File 17. Harry Golden Collection Part II. U of North Carolina at Charlotte.

King, Edward. Letter to Harry Golden. 13 Apr. 1961. Box 19 File 30. Harry Golden Collection Part II. U of North Carolina at Charlotte.

King, Martin Luther, Jr. Letter to Harry Golden. 2 Jul. 1962. Box 19 File 5. Harry Golden Collection Part II. U of North Carolina at Charlotte.

King, Martin Luther, Jr. Letter to Harry Golden. 30 Apr. 1964. Box 11 File 29. Harry Golden Collection Part II. U of North Carolina at Charlotte.

King, Martin Luther, Jr. Letter to Harry Golden. 3 Nov. 1964. Box 19 File 5. Harry Golden Collection Part II. U of North Carolina at Charlotte.

King, Martin Luther, Jr. Letter to Harry Golden. 15 Nov. 1965. Box 19 File 5. Harry Golden Collection Part II. U of North Carolina at Charlotte.

King, Martin Luther, Jr. Telegram to Harry Golden. 18 Mar. 1965. Box 11 File 19. Harry Golden Collection Part II. U of North Carolina at Charlotte.

King, Martin Luther, Jr. Telegram to Harry Golden. 7 Jul. 1966. Box 11 File 29. Harry Golden Collection Part II. U of North Carolina at Charlotte.

Koch, Edward. Letter to Harry Golden. 5 Feb. 1971. Box 20 File 17. Harry Golden Collection Part II. U of North Carolina at Charlotte.

Kornegay, Horace. Letter to Harry Golden. 15 Aug. 1961. Box 20 File 17. Harry Golden Collection Part II. U of North Carolina at Charlotte.

Kuchel, Thomas. Letter to Harry Golden. 3 Mar. 1965. Box 20 File 18. Harry Golden Collection Part II. U of North Carolina at Charlotte.

Laird, Melvin. Letter to Harry Golden. 17 Aug. 1964. Box 20 File 17. Harry Golden Collection Part II. U of North Carolina at Charlotte.

Lewis, Alfred Baker. Letter to Harry Golden. 14 Feb. 1962. Box 14 File 1. Harry Golden Collection Part II. U of North Carolina at Charlotte.

MacGregor, Clark. Letter to Harry Golden. 1 Oct. 1964. Box 20 File 17. Harry Golden Collection Part II. U of North Carolina at Charlotte.

McCarthy, Eugene. Letter to Harry Golden. 17 Nov. 1964. Box 20 File 18. Harry Golden Collection Part II. U of North Carolina at Charlotte.

McGee, Gale. Letter to Harry Golden. 1 Aug. 1966. Box 20 File 18. Harry Golden Collection Part II. U of North Carolina at Charlotte.

McGovern, George. Letter to Harry Golden. 12 Aug. 1972. Box 13 File 51. Harry Golden Collection Part II. U of North Carolina at Charlotte.

McGovern, George. Letter to Harry Golden. 23 Aug. 1972. Box 13 File 21. Harry Golden Collection Part II. U of North Carolina at Charlotte.

McGovern, George. Letter to William Goldhurst. 18 Feb. 1983. Harry Golden Collection. William Goldhurst Private Holdings, Gainesville, FL.

McGovern, George. "Remarks" for Harry Golden Day at the University of North Carolina at Charlotte. 9 Apr. 1973. Harry Golden Collection. William Goldhurst Private Holdings, Gainesville, FL.

Mantiband, Charles. Letter to Harry Golden. 2 Apr. 1960. Box 13 File 7. Harry Golden Collection Part II. U of North Carolina at Charlotte.

Mantiband, Charles. Letter to Harry Golden. 4 May 1963. Box 13 File 7. Harry Golden Collection Part II. U of North Carolina at Charlotte.

Mantiband, Charles. Letter to Harry Golden. 1 Sept. 1963. Box 13 File 7. Harry Golden Collection Part II. U of North Carolina at Charlotte.

Martin, Norman. Letter to Harry Golden. 15 Feb. 1973. Box 20 File 17. Harry Golden Collection Part II. U of North Carolina at Charlotte.

Minow, Newton. Letter to Harry Golden. 30 Aug. 1961. Box 13 File 36. Harry Golden Collection Part II. U of North Carolina at Charlotte.

Minow, Newton. Letter to Harry Golden. 10 Sept. 1962. Box 13 File 36. Harry Golden Collection Part II. U of North Carolina at Charlotte.

Mondale, Walter F. Letter to Harry Golden. 29 July 1976. Box 13 File 43. Harry Golden Collection Part II. U of North Carolina at Charlotte.

Mondale, Walter F. Letter to Harry Golden. 10 April 1980. Box 13 File 43. Harry Golden Collection Part II. U of North Carolina at Charlotte.

Morton, Rogers. Letter to Harry Golden. 27 Aug. 1964. Box 20 File 17. Harry Golden Collection Part II. U of North Carolina at Charlotte.

Murray, James. Letter to Harry Golden. 25 Mar. 1958. Box 20 File 18. Harry Golden Collection Part II. U of North Carolina at Charlotte.

Muskie, Edmund. Letter to Harry Golden. Mar. 1971. Box 13 File 51. Harry Golden Collection Part II. U of North Carolina at Charlotte.

Nixon, Richard. Telegram to Harry Golden. 18 May 1969. Box 2 File 37. Harry Golden Collection Part II. U of North Carolina at Charlotte.

Nixon, Richard. Letter to Harry Golden. 3 Nov. 1972. Harry Golden Collection Part II. U of North Carolina at Charlotte.

O'Hara, Barrat. Letter to Harry Golden. 11 Jul. 1961. Box 20 File 17. Harry Golden Collection Part II. U of North Carolina at Charlotte.

Pell, Claiborne. Letter to Harry Golden. 13 May 1962. Box 20 File 18. Harry Golden Collection Part II. U of North Carolina at Charlotte.

Roosevelt, Mrs. Franklin D. Letter to Harry Golden. 27 Mar. 1962. Box 17 File 31. Harry Golden Collection Part II. U of North Carolina at Charlotte.

Roosevelt, Mrs. Franklin D. Letter to Harry Golden. 30 June 1960. Box 17 File 31. Harry Golden Collection Part II. U of North Carolina at Charlotte.

Ribicoff, Abraham. Letter to Harry Golden. 21 Oct. 1966. Box 17 File 21. Harry Golden Collection Part II. U of North Carolina at Charlotte.

Ribicoff, Abraham. Letter to Harry Golden. 14 Oct. 1966. Box 17 File 21. Harry Golden Collection Part II. U of North Carolina at Charlotte.

Randolph, A. Phillip. Letter to Harry Golden. 28 Aug. 1970. Box 17 File 10. Harry Golden Collection Part II. U of North Carolina at Charlotte.

Reid, Ogden. Letter to Harry Golden. 29 April 1972. Harry Golden Collection. William Goldhurst Private Holdings, Gainesville, FL.

Randolph, A. Phillip. Letter to Harry Golden. 10 Sept. 1963. Box 17 File 10. Harry Golden Collection Part II. U of North Carolina at Charlotte.

Randolph, A. Phillip. Letter to Harry Golden. Jul. 1966. Box 17 File 10. Harry Golden Collection Part II. U of North Carolina at Charlotte.

Ryan, William. Letter to Harry Golden. 25 Jul. 1969. Box 8 File 27. Harry Golden Collection Part II. U of North Carolina at Charlotte.

Semans, Mary. Letter to Harry Golden. 19 Jul. 1979. Harry Golden Collection. William Goldhurst Private Holdings, Gainesville, FL.

Scott, Hugh. Letter to Harry Golden. 26 May 1964. Box 20 File 18. Harry Golden Collection Part II. U of North Carolina at Charlotte.

Secrest, Mac. Letter to Harry Golden. 24 Nov. 1964. Box 20 File 12. Harry Golden Collection Part II. U of North Carolina at Charlotte.

Taylor, Roy. Letter to Harry Golden. 14 Feb. 1973. Box 20 File 17. Harry Golden Collection Part II. U of North Carolina at Charlotte.

Truman, Harry. Letter to Harry Golden. 9 Mar. 1965. Box 19 File 64. Harry Golden Collection Part II. U of North Carolina at Charlotte.

Vivian, C.T. Letter to Harry Golden. 6 Oct. 1964. Box 19 File 5. Harry Golden Collection Part II. U of North Carolina at Charlotte.

Wachtel, Harry. Memorandum to American Foundation on Nonviolence Board of Directors. 26 Apr. 1966. Box 11 File 29. Harry Golden Collection Part II. U of North Carolina at Charlotte.

Walker, Wyatt Tee. Letter to Harry Golden. 2 Jul. 1962. Box 32 File 686. Harry Golden Collection Part I. U of North Carolina at Charlotte.

Walker, Wyatt Tee. Letter to Harry Golden. 6 Nov. 1963. Box 19 File 5. Harry Golden Collection Part II. U of North Carolina at Charlotte.

Walker, Wyatt Tee. Letter to Harry Golden. 4 May 1964. Box 19 File 5. Harry Golden Collection Part II. U of North Carolina at Charlotte.

Wilkins, Roy. Letter to Harry Golden. 13 May 1964. Box 14 File 1. Harry Golden Collection Part II. U of North Carolina at Charlotte.

Wilkins, Roy. Letter to George Abernathy. 16 June 1969. Box 14 File 1. Harry Golden Collection Part II. U of North Carolina at Charlotte.

Wilkins, Roy. Letter to Harry Golden. 6 Feb. 1961. Box 14 File 1. Harry Golden Collection Part II. U of North Carolina at Charlotte.

Wilkins, Roy. Letter to Harry Golden. 11 May 1963. Box 14 File 1. Harry Golden Collection Part II. U of North Carolina at Charlotte.

Wilkins, Roy. "Statement" for Harry Golden Day. 19 May 1969. Box 2 File 37. Harry Golden Collection Part II. U of North Carolina at Charlotte.

Yarborough, Ralph. Letter to Harry Golden. 9 Dec. 1964. Box 20 File 18. Harry Golden Collection Part II. U of North Carolina at Charlotte.

Zelenko, Herbert. Letter to Harry Golden. 13 June 1962. Box 20 File 17. Harry Golden Collection Part II. U of North Carolina at Charlotte.

Awards

Agudas and Beth Israel Brotherhoods. "Man of the Year" Plaque to Harry Golden. 14 April 1959. Awards Series Box 159. Harry Golden Collection Part I. U of North Carolina at Charlotte.

American Jewish Committee Anti-Defamation League. "Distinguished Journalism" Plaque to Harry Golden. 18 June 1959. Awards Series Box 159. Harry Golden Collection Part I. U of North Carolina at Charlotte.

Abraham Brith. "Grand Master Award" Plaque to Harry Golden. 27 June 1960. Awards Series Box 159. Harry Golden Collection Part I. U of North Carolina at Charlotte.

Carver College. Plaque to Harry Golden. May 1955. Awards Series Box 159. Harry Golden Collection Part I. U of North Carolina at Charlotte.

City Council, City of Chicago, Illinois. "A Resolution" on Harry Golden. 6 Oct. 1981. Harry Golden Collection. William Goldhurst Private Holdings, Gainesville, FL.

Elks Grand Lodge. "Lovejoy Award" Plaque to Harry Golden. 24 Aug. 1964. Awards Series Box 159. Harry Golden Collection Part I. U of North Carolina at Charlotte.

National Association for the Advancement of Colored People. "Hall of Fame" Plaque to Harry Golden. 23 May 1986. Awards Series Box 159. Harry Golden Collection Part I. U of North Carolina at Charlotte.

National Federation of Temple Brotherhoods. "Man of the Year" Plaque to Harry Golden. 15 Jan. 1959. Awards Series Box 159. Harry Golden Collection Part I. U of North Carolina at Charlotte.

National Newspaper Publishers Association. "Russwurm Award" Plaque to Harry Golden. 15 March 1958. Awards Series Box 159. Harry Golden Collection Part I. U of North Carolina at Charlotte.

Old North State Medical Society. Plaque to Harry Golden. 16 June 1965. Awards Series Box 159. Harry Golden Collection Part I. U of North Carolina at Charlotte.

Omega Psi Phi. Plaque to Harry Golden. 1 May 1960. Awards Series Box 159. Harry Golden Collection Part I. U of North Carolina at Charlotte.

P.S. 20 Alumni Association. Certificate to Harry Golden, 19 June 1959. Awards Series Box 159. Harry Golden Collection Part I. U of North Carolina at Charlotte.

Index

About the Author

Dr. Clarence Walter Thomas holds a Ph.D. in mass communications from the University of Florida, a M.S. in Television and Radio from Syracuse University, and a B.A. (with honors) in mass communications from Hampton Institute.

Dr. Thomas, a media historian, has taught for over eighteen years at colleges and universities in North Carolina, Florida, and Virginia. He is presently the Director of Graduate Studies at the School of Mass Communications, Virginia Commonwealth University. His next book explores the role of the press in the civil rights movement.